WHAT TO SAY *and* HOW TO SAY IT

"*What to Say and How to Say It* is pure gold for anyone hoping to have better, more fruitful conversations about these vitally important issues."

Holly Ordway
Author of *Apologetics and the Christian Imagination*

"In an insightful, practical, and very readable way, *What to Say and How to Say It* presents reasons for belief in God, and for several teachings rooted in reason and faith that our secular society rejects. I highly recommend it. This book fully delivers on what its title promises."

Cardinal Thomas Collins
Archbishop of Toronto

"Crisp and brisk, but never trite or brusque, this is a clear, useful, up-to-date guide that will help you defend the faith and address hot-button issues relating to sex, marriage, and identity. A book that is balanced, reasonable, practical, and, best of all, charitable—'speaking the truth in love.'"

Michael Ward
Coeditor of *The Cambridge Companion to C.S. Lewis*

"If you long to have charitable conversations about hot-button issues with friends and loved ones, this book is for you. If you want to be equipped to defend Church teaching with logical reasoning and avoid a heated argument, *What to Say and How to Say It* can be your guide. Brandon Vogt takes you step-by-step through some of the most emotionally charged topics of today so you can find common ground with those who disagree and communicate truth with clarity and kindness."

Haley Stewart
Author of *The Grace of Enough*

WHAT TO SAY *and* HOW TO SAY IT

Discuss Your Catholic Faith with Clarity and Confidence

BRANDON VOGT

A *ClaritasU* Book

AVE MARIA PRESS **AVE** Notre Dame, Indiana

Nihil Obstat:	Reverend Monsignor Michael Heintz, PhD
	Censor Librorum
Imprimatur:	Most Reverend Kevin C. Rhoades
	Bishop of Fort Wayne–South Bend
	Given at Fort Wayne, Indiana, on 20 October, 2019

The *Nihil Obstat* and *Imprimatur* are official declarations that a book or pamphlet is free of doctrinal or moral error. No implication is contained therein that those who have granted the *Nihil Obstat* or *Imprimatur* agree with its contents, opinions, or statements expressed.

Founded in 1865, Ave Maria Press is a ministry of the United States Province of Holy Cross.

www.avemariapress.com

Paperback: ISBN-13 978-1-59471-959-2

E-book: ISBN-13 978-1-59471-960-8

Special Edition product number: 30004

Cover and text design by Andy Wagoner.

Printed and bound in Canada.

Library of Congress Cataloging-in-Publication Data is available.

CONTENTS

INTRODUCTION

As a new Catholic, I was scared—really scared. I converted in college and went from knowing basically nothing about Catholicism to a confirmed Catholic, all within two years. I had read many books and went through RCIA, the year-long formation course for new Catholics. But when it came to talking about my new faith with other people, especially critics of Catholicism, I was afraid.

When family and friends learned of my conversion, they peppered me with all sorts of questions. Atheist friends laid into me, suggesting Catholicism was for mindless dupes who believed in God or went to church just because their parents told them to. Protestant friends began grilling me about the Eucharist, Mary, and the saints, saying Catholicism was all about rules and making you feel guilty. Other friends asked uncomfortable questions about the Church's positions on abortion, contraception, same-sex marriage, the sexual abuse crisis, the Bible, and much more.

And in most conversations, I didn't know what to say. I wasn't prepared. My RCIA classes were helpful in many respects, but we hardly touched on these prickly topics. So, when those issues came up in conversation, I was tongue-tied. I became so nervous and afraid. My typical reaction was just to hope the conversation would turn in a new direction so I wouldn't have to address those things.

On the rare occasions I did speak up, I inevitably said the wrong thing in the wrong way, and it made me feel even worse. I became convinced I was the most inadequate representative of Catholicism and that nobody would take the Catholic Church seriously after hearing me talk about it.

I'm guessing some of this sounds familiar to you. Who among us hasn't been nervous or tongue-tied when talking about their faith? Who among us hasn't shied away from controversial religious and moral topics?

The Pew Research Center recently polled thousands of adults across the country, from all different religions, asking, "What do you personally think is the best thing to do when someone disagrees with you about religion?"

They were given three choices:

1. Try to persuade the other person to change their mind (i.e., evangelize).
2. Try to understand the other person's belief but agree to disagree (i.e., just listen).
3. Avoid discussing religion (i.e., ignore the topic).

Around 67 percent of Americans chose the second option, to just listen. In other words, the large majority of us are fine hearing what other people think about religion, but we definitely don't want to share *our own* views, or defend those views.

Another 27 percent chose the third option, meaning they don't want to talk about religion *at all*. They prefer to just ignore it. They don't want to listen *or* speak about it. They're likely afraid the discussion will get heated or produce hurt feelings.

This leaves only 6 percent of Americans who chose the first option, meaning just 6 percent of adults are open to discussing their own religious beliefs and even, perhaps, trying to persuade other people to change their mind.

Now, as a Catholic who thinks the Catholic faith is true and that everyone should consider it—indeed, my last book was titled *Why I Am Catholic (and You Should Be Too)*—that number is depressingly low.

But the result gets even worse for us Catholics. When you filter the responses by religion, you find that only 2 percent of Catholics chose the first option. Among *all* religious groups, including nonreligious groups like atheists and agnostics, this put Catholics at the absolute bottom. In other words, Catholics are the *least likely* of any religious group to try to persuade people to change their mind about religion.

Just think about that: 98 percent of Catholics do *not* want to talk about their own religious views with people who disagree. Now, to be sure, most Catholics love their faith. We love the Mass and the sacraments. We love God. We embrace the Church's moral teachings. But for some reason, we're afraid of openly discussing these things with friends, family, and coworkers, especially those who reject Catholicism.

Why is that? Well, after struggling with this myself, and then talking with hundreds of other Catholics, I'm convinced it's because nobody taught us how to talk about these things. The parishes and ministries I experienced in my early Catholic years were wonderful. They helped me to encounter Jesus in the sacraments and to love him more deeply. They offered beautiful prayer experiences. But when it came to equipping me to talk with friends and family about the faith, especially about the hardest, hot-button issues, I just wasn't prepared. I never learned any real, practical strategies to discuss my faith in the normal, day-to-day world, with people who disagree.

I'm guessing your experience is the same. In our parishes and schools, we just don't find practical training on how to discuss the big, tough issues Catholics face today, such as atheism, evil and suffering, same-sex marriage, transgenderism, abortion, and more.

That's why I wrote this book. My goal is to get you clear about each of these subjects, because clarity breeds confidence. The more clearly you understand each topic, the more confident you'll be about it. And the more confident you are, the *more willing* and *happier* you'll be to discuss these things.

To help with this, a few years ago I created a new platform called ClaritasU, an online school and training ground for Catholics who want to learn how to effortlessly discuss these hard topics. More than four thousand people have signed up, including hundreds of priests, religious, seminarians, parents, and more. It's an exciting new movement with life-changing results.

One thing we've learned through ClaritasU is that to get clear on any particular issue, a Catholic just needs to master three things: first, the Catholic view of the topic; second, the best objections to the Catholic view; and third, how to answer those top objections.

That's it. When you're clear about those three things—what you believe, the best objections to those beliefs, and how to answer those objections—you're totally equipped and confident. You won't get rattled or tongue-tied. You can walk into almost any situation, whether a conversation with your children or a debate with friends, and know that you won't be nervous, you won't be afraid, and you'll stay cool and collected. You'll be confident, because you're clear about what to say and how to say it.

So, as we learn how to talk about each of these tough issues as Catholics, that's the format we'll follow in this book. For each topic, in each chapter, you'll first learn the Catholic view, then the best objections to that view (so you're not surprised by them), and finally how to respond to those objections.

In chapter 1, you'll learn the best strategies for talking with atheists, whether it's children who claim they no longer believe in God, or friends who make fun of your religious beliefs. You'll learn three simple arguments for God (and how to easily memorize them), as well as some tips for having more fruitful discussions with skeptics.

In chapter 2, we'll look at the problem of evil and suffering, the best objection to Christianity. Why is there so much suffering in the world? Why doesn't God do anything about it? You'll discover why this problem is actually three problems in one, and you'll find out how to talk about each one effectively.

In chapter 3, we'll focus on the Bible and why we can trust what it says about Jesus. Many skeptics today—I'm sure you know some—don't just *disagree* with Jesus: they're not convinced Jesus even *existed*, or that if he did, the Bible probably doesn't accurately convey what he said and did. This chapter will give you simple ways to respond to these objections and teach you how to show why the Bible is deeply reliable, especially in what it says about Jesus.

In chapter 4, we'll get clear on the Eucharist. Another recent study from the Pew Research Center found that only one-third of US Catholics believe what the Church teaches about the Eucharist, that the Eucharist is truly the Body and Blood of Christ. The rest believe it's just a symbol or something else. This survey affirms how desperately we need to get clear on what the Eucharist is and, just as important, how to explain it clearly to others—especially to non-Catholics. This chapter will show you how.

In chapter 5, we'll look at abortion. You'll learn the one key question you should return to in every conversation about abortion, which will make your discussions so much easier. You'll also discover how to talk about the so-called hard cases that abortion supporters bring up, such as rape, incest, or cases where the mother's health is in danger. If you're terrified of discussing abortion, don't worry: you'll feel totally different after reading this chapter.

In chapter 6, we'll study same-sex marriage, an issue that has gone from obscurity to mainstream in just a handful of years. How do you respond to common same-sex marriage slogans? How do you defend the traditional view of marriage? How do you talk about these things without seeming to be rigid and judgmental? You'll learn all that and more.

In chapter 7, the final chapter, we'll look at transgenderism, which has quickly become a central and divisive cultural issue. What are the key terms you need to know? What should you, as a Catholic, think of transgenderism? You'll learn those facts, plus several good questions and talking points to help you stay in the driver's seat when discussing the issue.

One final note: Earlier in this introduction I mentioned ClaritasU. Each of the chapters in this book is based on a video course we've offered at ClaritasU and has been adapted for this book. If you like the format of these chapters and the tips and strategies they include, you'll love ClaritasU, which offers even *more* tactics and resources on even *more* hot-button issues. Learn more and join the thousands of Catholics getting clear about their faith at ClaritasU.com.

Let's dive in!

1

ANSWERING ATHEISM

If you haven't felt pressured yet by atheism, you will soon. Atheism is one of the fastest-growing beliefs. The number of atheists and agnostics in America has quadrupled in the last two decades. Atheists have a tremendous influence, especially in the popular culture. From TV sitcoms and channels such as National Geographic and the History Channel to movies, music, and books and to classrooms across the country, the skeptical agenda is being pushed full force. It's causing more and more people to question things they've long taken for granted, such as their belief in God, the soul, and morality. Atheism is undoubtedly on the rise.

So, if it's not the case yet, you *will* soon have atheist friends or coworkers openly challenging your basic beliefs. You *will* soon have close family members who, despite being raised Christian, have started to doubt God's existence. And when that time comes, what are you going to do? What are you going to say? How are you going to bring *clarity* and show them that God is real?

If you don't have answers to those questions now, don't worry. Most Christians don't. But in this chapter, you'll discover the answers you need. You'll learn exactly what to say and how to say it. (Some of this chapter was adapted from content in my book *Why I Am Catholic* [Ave Maria Press, 2017]. I recommend that book if you want even more reasons to reject atheism in favor of theism.)

THE SHOCKING RISE OF ATHEISM

The first thing we need to do is get clear on our terms. Let's begin with a few definitions. Generally, people give three basic answers to the question "Does God exist?" If they say, "Yes, God exists," then we call those people theists. A theist is someone who believes in a personal God. Christians are theists, but so are Jews, Muslims, Mormons, and many others. By far, the overwhelming majority of people throughout history have been theists.

Second, if you asked someone, "Does God exist?" and they say, "No, God does not exist," then we would call that person an atheist. There's a lot of debate about how to define *atheist*, but for our purposes this definition will be fine: an atheist is someone who does not think God exists.

And if you asked someone, "Does God exist?" and they say, "I don't know," then we would call that person an agnostic. An agnostic is someone who just doesn't know either way—they can't make up their mind whether God exists or not.

As mentioned earlier, the number of atheists and agnostics in America has quadrupled in the last two decades. What's behind this rise? Why are so many people doubting God? There are a lot of reasons, but I will focus on just two major factors: the New Atheism and the internet.

The New Atheism

The New Atheism is a movement of scientists and writers spearheaded by Richard Dawkins (author of *The God Delusion*), the late Christopher Hitchens (author of *God Is Not Great*), Daniel Dennett (author of *Breaking the Spell*), and Sam Harris (author of *Letter to a Christian Nation*), each of whom has written best-selling books denouncing God. Their books are typically angry and caustic. They're not out to disprove religion so much as to mock religious faith and make it look ridiculous. They depict Christianity as silly, irrational, and even dangerous.

Each of these authors has been on the *New York Times* best-seller list. Their books are not obscure, self-published titles reaching a few hundred people. They've reached millions of readers. This New Atheism has become especially attractive to young people. It has flourished on college campuses, spawning atheist and skeptic student groups and aggressive campaigns to squash religion. So, the New Atheism is hugely responsible for the surge of unbelief.

The Internet

A second contributing factor is the internet. Thanks to the internet, atheists now have a place to spread their views without fear of social ostracism. Before the internet, people were generally uncomfortable criticizing religion, because they usually had to do it in person, and being recognized as a public atheist was troublesome. But with the internet, anyone can anonymously post antireligious YouTube videos or leave mean-spirited comments mocking religion. And they're doing it in droves. When surveys ask young atheists about what contributed to their skepticism, the internet typically appears near the top of the list. They absorbed YouTube debates or read a prominent atheist's blog and soon stopped believing in God.

But what is it they find so compelling? Few Catholics have interacted with more atheists than I have. In 2011, I started StrangeNotions.com, a website designed to be the central place of dialogue between Catholics and atheists. I thought it would reach a small number of people, but it quickly exploded in popularity. More than three million people have now visited the site to chat about the big questions of life, making Strange Notions the largest outreach to atheists in the history of the Catholic Church.

Through the website, I've interacted with thousands of skeptics online, and they've given me a lot of insight into the general phenomenon of people abandoning their faith. They doubt God for various reasons: some philosophical, some emotional, some moral, and some personal. Yet in my experience, the one thing they all have in common is a desire for truth. They don't want to believe in God just because it makes them feel good, or just because their family has always believed in God. They only want to believe in God *if it's true* that God exists. And to affirm that, they say, they need evidence.

IS THERE EVIDENCE FOR GOD?

Someone once asked the great atheist philosopher Bertrand Russell what he would say if he found himself standing before God on judgment day and God asked him, "Why didn't you believe in me?" Russell replied, "'I would say, 'Not enough evidence, God! Not enough evidence!'"[1] If you hang around skeptics or atheists long enough, you'll hear the same demand. People are open to God, if only there were enough evidence!

Now whenever a friend or family member suggests there's no evidence for God, don't get uptight. This is a good thing. When someone wants proof or evidence before they accept a belief, that's commendable. It means they aren't willing to believe something without support.

But in this case, we need to ask for clarification: What do they mean by evidence? Oftentimes what they really want is scientific evidence. In the realm of science, evidence refers to data you can see, hear, taste, touch, or smell—things that directly confirm or undermine a hypothesis. And in the context of science, such evidence has led to remarkable results.

However, what we might call physical evidence, or sensory evidence, isn't the *only* type of evidence in the world. There are many truths we cannot prove through physical evidence. For instance, we don't have physical evidence that life is meaningful, or that murder is wrong, or that the world around us is real and not just a simulation cooked up as it was in *The Matrix*. Of course, we know all of those things are true, but not because we've found physical evidence to support them.

The same holds for God. Whether you believe he exists or not, God is by definition immaterial and transcendent. He is immaterial because he is not composed of physical matter. He is not made of material stuff like you and me. God is transcendent because he exists beyond space and time. Since that's the case, when we're searching for God, we would not expect to find direct, physical, scientific evidence for his existence within space and time. It's not just that we haven't yet found such evidence, though it may exist. It's that such evidence is impossible, even in principle.

Here's a good example to illustrate this: Suppose you met a man who was an expert coin collector. He spent his days walking different beaches with his metal detector, hunting for rare coins, and he was very successful. He had found thousands of coins in his lifetime. Now suppose one day you told him about the greatest ancient artifact of all, the Holy Grail, the very cup used by Jesus Christ during the Last Supper. "What does it look like?" he might ask. "Well," you would say, "if *Indiana Jones and the Last Crusade* was any indication, it was not ornate or covered in gold. It was a simple wooden cup."

The collector, eager to find it, spends the next several years searching the deserts of the Middle East for the cup with his metal detector. Yet he comes up empty. He returns to you and says, "I've spent years looking for this wooden cup, but I can't find it! The metal detector picks up nothing. I can only conclude you were making the whole thing up.

The cup doesn't exist!" What would you then say? Your natural reply would be, "Well, of course you'd think that, since you're using the wrong tool for the job. A metal detector isn't going to find a wooden cup, whether the cup exists or not. You need a different way to seek the cup!"

There's a parallel here with God. We can have no direct, scientific evidence for God. We're not going to find one of God's hairs, or detect his footprint, or run a scientific experiment to see if he exists.

But does that mean it's impossible to demonstrate God exists? No. It simply means that science isn't the right tool, just as the metal detector isn't the right tool to find a wooden cup. We need other tools when exploring nonscientific questions.

What other tools are there, besides science? One such tool is philosophy. Philosophy is concerned with life's biggest topics, from morality to meaning to God. It allows us to probe realities that can't be detected through our senses, which makes it a really good way to explore the evidence for God.

And that brings us to the main question: Is there any evidence for God? Many people certainly think so. But again, it's a different kind of evidence. Much of it takes the form of arguments for God. In fact, thinkers have identified no less than twenty arguments for God, arguments that range from the clear and simple to the extremely complex. Some of the arguments appeal to emotion or history, others to reason and experience.

We can approach the God question from many angles, and there's no one best way, but some of the arguments are stronger than others. In this book we'll look at three of the best arguments for God.

However, before we explore them, I want to note that if terms like *arguments* or *evidence* rub you the wrong way, you might instead consider these three arguments as *clues* that converge and point to a common conclusion, much like road signs guide you to a specific destination. A sign doesn't prove that the destination exists, but it does point the way. That's exactly what these arguments are—signposts to God. So, let's look at each of them, beginning with one of the simplest yet most powerful arguments for God.

THE KALAM ARGUMENT

The Kalam argument dates back to the Middle Ages but has been made popular today by William Lane Craig, an Evangelical Christian philosopher. It's one of the most famous arguments for God.

The argument is very simple. In fact, it's probably the easiest one to memorize. It has two premises and one conclusion. It runs like this:

Premise 1: Everything that begins to exist has a cause.
Premise 2: The universe began to exist.
Conclusion: The universe has a cause.

If you can memorize these three simple statements, you'll be well equipped when dialoguing with any skeptic.

Let's unpack each of those three statements.

The First Premise

This statement says everything that begins to exist has a cause. It's very important that we get this right. Some atheists try to refute the Kalam argument by responding, "Ah! Well, if everything that exists has a cause, and God exists, then what caused God?" But the premise does not claim, "Everything that *exists* has a cause." It says, "Everything that *begins to exist* has a cause." Since God—by definition, and whether you believe in him or not—is eternal and never began to exist, this first premise wouldn't apply to him. Therefore, the rhetorical question "What caused God?" is like asking, "Whom is the bachelor married to?" or "What caused the uncaused being?" Those questions would be senseless even if no bachelors existed, or if there were no uncaused beings. It's just a confusion of terms.

Now that we've cleared away that misunderstanding, let's turn back to the first premise. Is it true? Does everything that begins to exist have a cause? For most people, the answer is yes, and it's common sense. Almost nobody denies it. The statement simply means that nothing just springs into existence, randomly and without a cause. For if things did come into being that way, then our world would be a wild spree of things popping into existence like magic. Only it would be worse than magic, since with magic you at least have a magician who pulls rabbits out of a hat. But in a world that violated this first premise, you'd get rabbits popping in and out of being even without magicians or hats or any other causes. Few sane people believe the world works this way. So, through experience and reflection nearly all of us agree that everything that begins to exist has a cause.

The Second Premise

This premise says that the universe began to exist. This claim is slightly more controversial than the first one, or at least it used to be. For centuries, most scientists believed that the universe was eternal—that it had always existed in the past. This conveniently avoided ascribing a beginning to the universe, which would have implied a creation moment. But over the last hundred years, from the Big Bang theory to new discoveries in quantum cosmology, science has produced a stunning reversal. Today, the scientific consensus is that the universe did have a beginning roughly fourteen billion years ago.

Alexander Vilenkin, a leading non-Christian cosmologist, was invited to speak at a colloquium for Stephen Hawking's seventieth birthday. There, in front of the greatest scientists in the world, Vilenkin confirmed, "All the evidence we have says that the universe had a beginning."[2] It's rare for scientists to speak with this measure of conclusiveness, but Vilenkin affirms it's not just that *some* of the evidence points to a beginning of the universe, or even the *majority* of evidence, but that *all* of the evidence points that way today.

The Third Premise

So, the first two premises are widely accepted today: everything that begins to exist has a cause, and the universe began to exist. If that's the case, then the third statement, the conclusion of the argument, logically follows. We cannot avoid it. If everything that begins to exist has a cause, and the universe began to exist, then the universe must have had a cause.

The Evidence for God

That leads us to wonder, What is the cause of the universe? It certainly couldn't have been anything within the universe or even the universe itself, since things can't cause themselves to come into existence. That defies logic. It would be like saying your arm caused *you* to come into existence. That couldn't be, since before you existed, there was no arm!

So, the cause of the universe must be something *beyond* the universe, something beyond all matter, energy, space, and time. In other words, it must be transcendent (beyond the universe), it must be immaterial (beyond matter and space), it must be eternal (beyond time), and if it created something so massively complex as the universe, it must be tremendously powerful and intelligent. Well, a transcendent, immaterial, eternal, supremely powerful, and intelligent cause of the universe—what does that sound like to you?

Now, this proof for God is fairly abstract. It can be a little difficult to understand, at least at first. It doesn't generate the warm, personal faith you might derive from prayer. And it doesn't prove the fullness of God, especially things we only know because God has revealed them to us, such as that God is love or is a Trinity of persons.

But the Kalam argument does present a substantial slice of God, a slice far too thick for any atheist to accept. So, commit right now to memorizing these three simple statements:

1. Everything that begins to exist has a cause.
2. The universe began to exist.
3. The universe has a cause.

If you can memorize and recall these statements, you'll have an extremely powerful argument for God, always at the ready whenever someone challenges your faith.

THE CONTINGENCY ARGUMENT

Although I like the Kalam argument a lot, my favorite case for God is one known as the contingency argument. It's a little more complex, but I think it's a bit stronger.

Here's a simple version: Everything that exists does so in one of two ways. It's either contingent, which means it depends on something else for its existence, or necessary, which means it has to exist and doesn't depend on anything else.

Consider some concrete examples: tables, rocks, animals, mountains, iPhones, and shirts are all contingent. They don't have to exist, and they could have existed in other ways, colors, shapes, or forms. People are contingent too. As much as we'd like to think we're necessary, the fact is we're not. All of us come into existence and go out of existence. We didn't have to come into being. The fact that we could have *not* existed makes us contingent. We depended on our parents to bring us into being, and we depend on many other factors such as food, water, and oxygen to stay in existence. That's why philosophers say we are not just contingent—we are *radically* contingent, contingent to our very core.

But that leads to a question: Isn't everything contingent? Doesn't everything depend on something else to come into existence or to stay in existence? The answer is no. It couldn't be the case that everything is contingent. Think about it. If everything were contingent, then A would depend on B, B would depend on C, C would depend on D, and so on. But this couldn't go on forever. If the chain of contingent beings never had a first link, then nothing would ultimately exist. The chain needs to have at least one link that is necessary, not contingent. In other words, it needs at least one being that exists by itself, that doesn't depend on anything else to give it existence or keep it in existence.

Let me illustrate all this with another example. It comes from Peter Kreeft, and it's the best way I know to explain the contingency argument to friends and family.

Suppose I tell you about a special book that explains everything you ever want to know. We might call it the Big Book of Explanations. You obviously want that book very much because you're desperate to discover what explains everything. So, you ask me whether I have the Big Book of Explanations.

I say, "No, I don't have it. I can let you borrow it, but I have to get it from my wife." "Well, does she have it?" "No, she has to get it from her neighbor." "Does he have it?" "No, he has to get it from his teacher, who has to get it from so-and-so."

Now, if nobody actually has the book, then you will never get it. It doesn't matter how long or short the chain of borrowers is, whether it's two people, a hundred people, or a billion people. You will only get the book if there is someone at the beginning of the chain who actually has the book, someone who doesn't need to borrow it from anyone else.

Existence is like that book. It is handed down the chain of causes. You and I got our existence from someone else, who got their existence from someone else, who got their existence from someone else, and so on. All of us have received our existence from something or someone outside of us. But this can't be the case for *every* being in the chain. If everyone borrowed existence from something else, then just as in our book example, we would never actually receive existence.

But we did receive it. We have existence; you and I exist. This means that no matter how long the chain of existence is, something, at some point, must have had existence in itself without borrowing it from someone else. In other words, there must have been a self-existent being, a necessary First Cause of existence. And this is precisely what thinkers for thousands of years, from Plato to Plotinus to Thomas Aquinas, have called God. That's the contingency argument in a nutshell.

Now, there are two reasons I like this argument even more than the Kalam argument. First, instead of dealing with the origin of the whole universe, it begins with just a single, contingent thing like you or me and says, "This one thing is contingent. So where did it come from? Well, it came from another contingent thing, and so on." Eventually, you reason there must have been a necessary cause responsible for all these contingent beings; otherwise they would never exist. That's what makes the contingency argument so strong—its simple, humble starting point.

I also like it better than the Kalam argument because it doesn't depend on the age of the universe. The Kalam argument's second premise says that the universe began to exist. Right now this isn't a problem, as almost all scientists agree that the universe had a beginning. But as we all know, science can change. The consensus sometimes shifts, and if tomorrow scientists determined the universe was actually infinitely old, the Kalam argument's second premise would become weaker.

The contingency argument is different. It doesn't depend on science, or on the universe's age. The universe could be six thousand years old, as some Fundamentalist Christians believe. It could be 13.7 billion years old, as most scientists believe. Or it could be infinitely old, as some atheists still believe. It doesn't matter for the contingency argument. Regardless of how old the universe is, it is still contingent and full of contingent things, and those things still require an explanation for why they exist. The only conclusion is there must be some explanation outside the universe, some necessary being or necessary cause that explains itself. And that's what we call God.

Both the Kalam and the contingency arguments demonstrate the existence of God from two different angles. But they don't tell us much about *what* that God is like. That's why we need to add one more powerful argument to the mix.

THE MORAL ARGUMENT

What is right and wrong? We humans have been asking that question since our earliest days, and we've seen all sorts of answers. People have many different views about how to be a good person. However, for the sake of this argument, we're interested not so much in *which* moral framework is correct but in the simple fact that almost all people agree there exists some moral standard that each of us is obliged to follow.

Moral Values and Duties

Few people say, "It doesn't matter whether you're good or bad, or whether you follow your conscience." Even the most hardened skeptic who thinks morality is just an illusion will get mad if you punch him in the nose or steal his wallet. He'll still say, "Hey, that's wrong! Why did you do that?"

For more proof of this, just look at young children. Even toddlers understand the idea of rights. They shout, "Mine! Mine! Mine!" and get upset when another child takes their toys. There's a basic moral sense that seems innate within us humans.

I live in Orlando, near Disney World, so I often see another example. Go to Disney, to any of the hour-long lines snaking around the attractions. Then skip ahead in line and see how people react. Even when someone skips accidentally, the moral policing is sharp and quick: "Hey, what are you doing? You can't do that it. We've been waiting here for hours! Get to the back of the line!" We all experience an inborn sense that some acts are just right, and some acts are just wrong. We all know there is such a thing as right and wrong, what we might call moral values.

In addition to moral values, we also experience moral duties. It's not just that we see certain actions as right or wrong; it's that we feel compelled to *do* the right actions and *avoid* the wrong ones. An invisible law seems to guide our behavior. Something inside us, around us, or beyond us serves as a moral authority, constantly reminding us of the way we ought to live. Those thoughts ("you *ought* to do this, you *ought not* to do that") are what we call moral duties.

Objective Morality

So, we have moral values and moral duties. The moral values tell us what is right and wrong, and the moral duties tell us that we ought to do the right thing. Those are the first two steps of the moral argument. The third step is to realize that at least some of these values and duties are objective. That is, they don't depend on personal feeling, preference, or opinion.

For example, all sane people agree it is morally wrong to torture young children for fun. We can all agree that we *ought not* to do this under any circumstance; there is nothing that could ever justify it. This is an objective fact. It's not one person's opinion that torturing children is wrong, or a moral fashion that may change over time. It's true at all times, for all people, yesterday, today, and forever. If we were to meet someone who thinks torturing children is fine, we wouldn't say, "Ah, that's OK. He has his moral opinions and we have ours." No, we would say that person is emphatically wrong and that he's deeply misguided, probably psychologically disturbed.

It's true that some people throughout history have been mistaken about objective moral facts, such as the wrongness of slavery or torture. But it's only because these things are objectively wrong that we're able to look back and acknowledge that those people *were mistaken*. If moral values and duties were just subjective and dependent on personal beliefs or on the feelings of the majority of people, then we would have no ground on which to criticize past moral mistakes.

But we do and are able to say, "Even though those people thought slavery was fine, they were wrong. Slavery was objectively wrong two thousand years ago, two hundred years ago, and is still wrong today, even if some people were confused about that throughout time."

With all that in mind, we've now confirmed three things. First, we all have moral values—we all believe that some things are good and other things are bad. Second, we all experience moral duties—we all know we should do the good things and avoid the bad ones, even if we sometimes fall short of that goal. And third, at least some of these moral values and duties are objective—in other words, they aren't just personal preferences, such as our favorite type of music or ice cream, but are real, objective features of reality.

The Moral Lawgiver

If all of that is true, and almost all people believe it is, then we must ask ourselves, Where do these objective moral values and duties come from? If there's a moral duty that seems to bind all of humanity, what or who gives it that authority? Or to put it more simply, if we have a moral law, where is the moral lawgiver?

Now, there are logically only three possibilities. These moral values and duties come from within us humans, they come from nature around us, or they come from something beyond nature, from a transcendent source. Let's look at each option.

From Humans?

Can these objective morals come from us humans? The answer is no because people are ultimately subjective. People's opinions change, and their moral moods shift. It's therefore impossible for individuals or groups to offer an unchanging standard by which to measure our moral performance.

We can see this, for example, with Nazi Germany. If moral values and duties simply stem from society and human opinion, then we would have no basis to condemn the horrible Nazi atrocities, other than saying, "I personally didn't like them." Or to use another example, even if the large majority of people believed slavery was acceptable, it's still wrong. Therefore objective morality can't derive from us humans.

From Nature?

Couldn't nature tell us how to behave? The answer is no again, since as the famous atheist David Hume noted, nature only shows us what *is*; it doesn't tell us how something *ought* to be (this is the famous "is-ought" problem in philosophy). For instance, nature can confirm that whenever we punch someone in the nose, it will cause them pain—that's the *is*. When you do *this*, *that* happens. However, nature cannot tell us that we *ought not* to cause others pain. That's a moral fact that we must get from somewhere else.

Some atheists suggest that morality may be derived from evolution. But evolution suffers from the same problem. It may show which moral behaviors lead to survival. For example, making friends is more conducive to survival than making enemies. But it doesn't bind us to act in a certain way. Evolution doesn't require that we ought to make friends and avoid enemies, or even that we ought to pursue survival above all else. Those are moral assumptions that we get from somewhere else.

From a Transcendent Source?

So where do we get morality? In the end we're left with one plausible explanation. Morality must come from something beyond humans and beyond nature. It must come from a transcendent source of goodness. That's what we call God.

Even atheists admit this implicitly. Richard Dawkins, perhaps the world's most famous atheist, has written that if atheism were true, there would be "no evil and no good, nothing but blind, pitiless indifference."[3] In other words, without God, there would be no objective morality. But we do have objective moral values and duties! Therefore, God must exist.

This explanation makes sense of all the evidence. Why do we experience innate moral values, even as toddlers? Because we were created by God, the all-perfect source of goodness, who gave us an innate knowledge of right and wrong. To use biblical language, God's moral law was "written on our hearts." This explains why even people who don't believe in God feel obliged to follow moral rules and can still lead impressive moral lives.

Why do we face moral duties? Because God has created us with a specific plan about how we ought to behave in order to live a good life that produces happiness. Why are these values and duties objective? Because they're grounded in God, who is an unchanging source. God doesn't bend and fluctuate like nature, society, or personal opinion. He is an objective standard.

If you want to put the moral argument in a way that's easy to memorize, we might sum it up like this:

Premise 1: If God does not exist, objective morality does not exist.
Premise 2: Objective morality does exist.
Conclusion: Therefore, God exists.

The conclusion logically follows if both premises are true. So, you want to focus on those two premises.

There are two good reasons to believe premise 1. First, almost all atheists admit this is true, including Richard Dawkins, in the quote we shared earlier. Other leading atheists such as Michael Ruse and the late J. L. Mackie affirm this too. Also, all the natural alternatives on which to ground objective morality, such as humans, society, or nature, won't work because they're all subjective. They change and fluctuate, so they can't be objective. There is atheistic ground for objective morality.

We know the second premise is true too—that objective morality does exist—through our own experience and moral intuition. Most sane people believe in objective morality. There are, admittedly, some who say they don't believe in it, but even they will get angry when you do something immoral to them, betraying their belief that morality is just a matter of personal sentiment. At their core, they really believe at least some moral values and duties are objective.

So that's the short form of the moral argument. It's a good argument for God as it shows how our sense of right and wrong ultimately point to a transcendent source of morality that we call God. Also, it doesn't just tell us *that* God exists; it tells us something *about* him and what he's like. God must be the embodiment or source of moral goodness, which is why theists consider God to be all-good or perfect.

Expert Interview with Robert Spitzer, S.J.

➤ **Watch the interview here: https://claritasu.com/spitzer**

Fr. Robert Spitzer is a well-known Catholic priest who specializes in the philosophy of science, metaphysics, and the existence of God. He's the founder and president of the Magis Center, which produces documentaries, books, curricula, and new media materials to show the close connection between faith and reason.

In this interview, Fr. Spitzer responds to the following questions:

1. Why do you think atheism has surged in popularity, especially among young people?
2. Why was the formulation of the Big Bang theory such a momentous event when it comes to God?
3. How does the remarkable fine-tuning of the universe demonstrate the existence of God?
4. How would you condense the best evidence for God into a few simple talking points?

Excerpt from the Interview

"If God is outside the universe, then how in the world are you going to use evidence from inside the universe to disprove an entity when it's completely beyond the universe? It cannot be done any more than a cartoon character can assemble all of the elements of his cartoon to disprove the cartoonist." (Fr. Robert Spitzer)

TIPS FOR TALKING WITH ATHEISTS

Now that we've got the arguments in hand, I want to share some easy tips and tactics to use when talking with atheists. I've sharpened many of these approaches in my years running StrangeNotions.com, learning what it takes to have a fruitful conversation.

Tip 1: Respect their intelligence.

Some people think atheism is so ridiculous and so incomprehensible that they openly mock or belittle those who question God. Don't make that mistake. Most atheists I've met are smart, sincere, and good-hearted. And even if they're not, treat them as if they are. Don't talk down to them or be condescending, the way you might to a child. Treat them with respect and compliment their intelligence. When you do, they'll be much more likely to hear what you have to say.

Tip 2: Find common ground.

If you're talking with a skeptic, you likely disagree about God and religion. So, don't start there. Instead, focus on areas of agreement. Maybe you both appreciate the value of science. Start with that. Hopefully you both value critical thinking and believe we should follow the evidence wherever it leads. Begin there. You want to start any conversation on a good foot, and finding common ground will do just that.

Tip 3: Ask good questions.

Instead of trying to shove your view on an atheist friend, sit back and ask questions about what *they* believe. This will both help you to understand where they're coming from and force them to clarify exactly what they believe.

There are two questions I love to raise with an atheist. First, I like to ask, "Which argument for God do you find *strongest*, and why does it fail?" Or to ask it another way, "What's the *best* reason to believe in God, and why doesn't it convince you?" This puts them on the spot—not in a bad way but in a way that causes them to reflect on whether they've actually considered the God question fairly and thoroughly enough.

In my experience, few atheists have actually read books defending God or have studied the issue at length. Therefore, they'll usually respond by referencing a relatively poor argument or reason, one that even you and I would reject. When they do, you can kindly reply, saying, "Oh? Is that the best reason you can think of? I can think of several better reasons to believe in God . . . ," and then roll out one of the three arguments we treated in this chapter.

Another strategy is to ask, "What would it take for you to believe in God?" This question will help reveal whether the person is genuinely open to God or whether they're so closed, demanding such a high standard of evidence, that it could never be met. When I ask atheists this question, I'll sometimes hear, "Well, I guess I'd believe in God if he appeared right in front of me and told me he existed, or if he wrote something in the stars such as 'My name is God and I exist.'" The problem with answers like that, as you can point out, is that such displays might be surprising and extraordinary, but even if they occurred, a skeptic could still find some way to explain them away. For example, maybe the skeptic was just hallucinating when he encountered someone claiming to be God. Maybe what looked like writing in the stars was actually a light projection from some prankster or government experiment. Experiences like this can always be explained away. So, if these are the sort of answers you get, push back a little and suggest we really need a higher and more convincing reason to believe in God, something like a philosophical argument. And then again, roll out one of the three philosophical arguments that we covered in this chapter.

RECOMMENDED BOOKS
(in order of importance)

Trent Horn, *Answering Atheism: How to Make the Case for God with Logic and Charity* (Catholic Answers Press, 2013).

A comprehensive consideration of atheist arguments and a clear, persuasive presentation of the Christian evidence for God. A book you can share with an atheist who will appreciate Horn's respectful treatment of their arguments.

William Lane Craig, *Reasonable Faith* (Crossway, 2008).

Craig, an Evangelical philosopher, presents an overall defense of the reasonableness of Christianity, including a thoroughgoing explanation of the main arguments for God's existence.

William Lane Craig, *On Guard: Defending Your Faith with Reason and Precision* (David C. Cook, 2010).

A popular presentation of the arguments for God that includes outlines mapping out possible conversations with atheists.

Edward Feser, *The Last Superstition: A Refutation of the New Atheism* (St. Augustine Press, 2010).

An in-depth explanation of Thomas Aquinas's five proofs for God undergirded with the philosophy behind them. Not a book to give to atheists as Feser is somewhat polemical, but a good book for Catholics to read.

Matt Fradd, *20 Answers: Atheism* (Catholic Answers Press, 2014).

A quick-read booklet that gives accessible answers to questions about atheist arguments.

FOR REFLECTION AND DISCUSSION

1. What are two prominent reasons atheism is surging today?
2. What can you say when someone says to you, "There's no evidence for God!"?
3. Why doesn't the reply "What caused God?" refute the Kalam argument?
4. In your own words, explain the argument from contingency.

5. Why is the contingency argument stronger than the
   Kalam argument?
6. How does the objectivity of moral values and duties
   demonstrate the existence of God?
7. What are some effective ways of carrying on a conversation with an atheist?

FOR PRACTICE

For each of the following scenarios, write a response using
what you learned in this chapter.

1. You're speaking with an atheist who says, "There's
   just no evidence for God's existence. I need evidence
   before I believe something. I am a rational skeptic.
   Give me evidence for God, and I'll believe."
2. An unbeliever says to you, "I believe in science. There
   is no direct scientific evidence supporting the existence of God. Why should I believe something so
   unscientific?" (Respond by clarifying the type of evidence we have for God and referencing a philosophical argument.)

2

EVIL AND SUFFERING

They're three of the most heartbreaking words we hear—
Where was God? A massive hurricane or tsunami kills
thousands—Where was God? School shootings or terrorist
attacks claim dozens of innocent lives—Where was God? A
loved one learns he or she has cancer or another terrible disease—Where was God? A young child passes away shortly
after being born—Where was God?

Intense suffering naturally causes us to wonder why
God doesn't do anything to stop it. Why does he allow
evil, pain, and suffering to flourish? People have been asking these questions for thousands of years. In fact, the old-
est book of the Bible, the book of Job, written sometime
between 600 and 400 BC, focuses precisely on this problem.
Job, who is described as "a blameless and upright man,"
experiences one tragedy after another.

First, enemies come and steal his oxen and donkeys and
kill many of his servants. Then fire falls from the sky and
wipes out his sheep (along with more servants). Then new
enemies come and cause more damage and death. Then a
tornado whips across the desert and smashes the house,
where all of his sons and daughters are eating, killing them
all. Can you imagine? Within a handful of hours Job loses

all of his animals, all of his servants, his house, and all of his children. Oh, and then for good measure, Job also begins suffering from boils, a terrible skin disease. Naturally, he wonders—Where was God? Why did God allow this to happen?

In this chapter, we'll focus on that question, commonly known as the problem of evil or the problem of pain and suffering. There's no easy answer to this difficult problem, but Christianity does offer a way forward, and you'll learn how to discuss this tough issue with friends and family.

First, we'll look more closely at the problem and understand why St. Thomas Aquinas considered it the number-one objection to Christianity. Then we'll break apart the problem into three separate issues: first the logical problem of evil, then the evidential problem of evil, and finally the emotional problem of evil. It's important to distinguish these three subissues because they're really three different problems that require three different ways of addressing them.

We'll also study some of the best objections related to the problem of evil, so that when you hear them among friends and family, you'll know exactly what to say.

Finally, some key talking points and tips will sum up the chapter, so you'll be ready for conversations whenever the topic comes up.

THE BEST OBJECTION TO CHRISTIANITY

St. Thomas Aquinas is best known for his massive *Summa Theologiae* (Summary of Theology), which is a lengthy collection of articles and arguments. It spans more than three thousand pages in its most popular edition. Many people consider Aquinas the brightest mind in the whole Catholic tradition. But the *Summa* doesn't just contain Aquinas's own thoughts and arguments, and he doesn't list everything that Catholics believe. Instead, he conducts a back-and-forth exchange. He begins with a topic or question and then first considers the best objections to his view on the matter. He usually states the objections so clearly and forcefully that he makes his opponents' case even better than they do.

Then, in each article of the *Summa*, Aquinas responds to those objections, showing where they fail, before finally offering and defending his own view. This is the rhythm of his entire *Summa*: objections, responses, and then an explanation of his view. Aquinas usually handles three or four objections to each position, but in the most famous article in the entire book, the one on the existence of God, he only offers two objections.

The article is titled "Whether God Exists?" Note, by the way, that Aquinas doesn't assume in the beginning of his book that God exists and move on from there. He begins by questioning whether God exists at all. It's a sign of his intellectual humility that he's willing to debate even the most fundamental questions.

In this article—part 1, question 2, article 3 of the *Summa*—Aquinas asks whether God exists, and then he observes that there are only two good reasons to believe God does *not* exist.

One reason he gives is that we can explain everything in the natural world without referring to God, so why need him? It doesn't seem that God is necessary to explain lightning, airplanes, mountains, or the diversity of species. We have natural explanations for all those things, so therefore God is unnecessary. This is a decent objection, though Aquinas does refute it a few lines later.

But that's not the one we'll focus on here. Most important is the other objection he offers, and it's the first one he lists. This presumably means Aquinas thinks this is the biggest and most important reason to deny God. The objection is the problem of evil and suffering. Here's how Aquinas says it: "It seems that God does not exist; because if one of two contraries be infinite, the other would be altogether destroyed. But the word 'God' means that He is infinite goodness. If, therefore, God existed, there would be no evil discoverable; but there is evil in the world. Therefore, God does not exist."

That's a pithy way to sum up the problem of evil. Aquinas says that you can't have two infinite, contrary things. If one is infinite, the other would be destroyed. For example, if people were infinitely nice, they would have no meanness in them—not even a little. Their meanness would have been destroyed.

That's the principle. Take two contrary things, and if one is infinite, the other must be destroyed or absent. Aquinas applies this principle to God. We Christians say that God, among other things, is infinitely good. But if this is true, then the opposite of goodness—namely, evil—should not exist at all. Yet we know from personal experience that there is evil in the world. There's the Holocaust, terrorist bombings, tsunamis, hurricanes, murders, and more. If there's one thing we're absolutely sure of, it's that evil does exist.

But if evil exists, then there must not be a contrary infinite. If evil exists, God must not be infinitely good. That, in a nutshell, is Aquinas's objection that he thinks is the biggest, strongest objection to God. It's the best argument in the atheist's toolbox.

Aquinas, of course, isn't the only one to express this problem of evil. Historians trace it at least back to the fifth century BC to the Greek philosopher Epicurus. He framed the problem in this way, in the words of David Hume:

> Is God willing to prevent evil, but not able? Then he is impotent.
>
> Is he able, but not willing? Then he is malevolent.
>
> Is he both able and willing? Whence then is evil?
>
> Is he neither able nor willing? Then why call him God?[1]

That's another pithy way to form the problem. Here's one more formulation. Critics offer three statements:

> God is all-good.
> God is all-powerful.
> Evil exists in the world.

The critic then claims that all three of these statements can't be true at the same time. At best, only two of them can be true. For example, the critic says if God is all-good, but evil exists, then he must not be all-powerful. Or the critic says, perhaps God is all-powerful and yet evil exists, which must mean God is not all-good. Or finally, the critic says, maybe God is all-good and all-powerful, but in that case God would want to stop evil and be powerful enough to do it, so evil cannot actually exist—it's just an illusion.

But we know that evil, pain, and suffering do exist in the world. It's an empirical fact. Although some religions, like Buddhism, try to solve the problem by suggesting evil is illusory, virtually all people know from experience this isn't true. Evil is very real, and its presence can be seen and felt every day.

That, in a nutshell, is the problem of evil. It's the best objection to God, and therefore the best objection to Christianity. It's also one of the hardest things to discuss, especially when the person in front of you has experienced some deep evil, pain, or suffering.

THE THREEFOLD PROBLEM OF EVIL

But as we noted earlier, the problem of evil is really three different problems packed into one: the logical problem, the evidential problem, and the emotional problem.

The Logical Problem of Evil

People struggling with this problem believe that there is a logical contradiction between the idea of an all-good, all-powerful God and the presence of evil. They say that only one of those two things can exist, but not both. A good summary of the logical problem of evil says it's logically impossible for God and evil to coexist.

The Evidential Problem of Evil

This takes a more modest approach, admitting that there may not be a logical contradiction between God and evil but that there is just *so much* evil in the world, it outweighs any reasons God could have for allowing it. Thus, the evidential problem suggests that in light of all this evil, it's possible, but extremely unlikely, that God exists.

For example, someone struggling with this problem might say, "Look at how much evil was involved in the Holocaust! What good came out of it? Maybe a little? In any case, the evil so outweighed the good that there must not be an all-good, all-powerful God."

The Emotional Problem of Evil

This problem is focused less on intellectual concerns and more on the personal, agonizing, subjective experience of pain and suffering. For example, consider the poor mother who loses an infant son to a sudden terminal disease. Or the child who prays and prays for her grandmother to be healed yet still sees her pass away. Or consider the pain and suffering you yourself have experienced.

In such cases, intellectual answers fail to satisfy. They don't really solve our problem. We still feel deep pain and confusion. And in the face of such darkness we're tempted to doubt that God exists or cares about our struggles.

Although all three problems touch on the problem of evil and suffering, they're unique, and each one needs to be handled differently. So let's take them one at a time.

THE LOGICAL PROBLEM OF EVIL

Is there a logical contradiction between an all-good, all-powerful God and the existence of evil? The short answer is no. Why? Because God could have good reasons for permitting certain evils and suffering, perhaps in order to bring about greater goods. And if it's even *possible* that God could have reasons for permitting evil, then there's no logical contradiction between God and evil.

Let me give you an example. Most of us go to the dentist regularly, but I've yet to meet a single person who actually enjoys it. It's something we know we have to do, but it's not pleasurable. It's invariably uncomfortable, often painful. The dentist sticks sharp metal tools and spinning discs in your mouth and pokes and scrapes against your teeth and gums. It's a time of suffering. But we permit that pain in order to bring about the greater good of healthy teeth. Similarly, God permits certain acts of evil and suffering because through them he can bring about greater goods.

But what kind of goods? For example, what good would possibly justify something like the Holocaust? One answer is free will. It's one of the most extraordinary gifts we've been given, the power to freely choose how to act.

We know that free will means we can choose good or evil, and when faced with such a choice, we often choose poorly. Of course, God could simply prevent us from ever choosing evil, but think about what that would mean. If we could never really choose evil, then our freedom is not real freedom. True freedom requires saying yes or no, choosing good or evil, without constraint.

The Holocaust was a moral evil, which means it was the product of many morally bad choices—egregiously bad choices—by many characters, Hitler most notably. God, of course, could have prevented Hitler and other Nazis from choosing evil. But again, that would have compromised the gift of human freedom, and that's just too high a price to pay.

But this brings us to an important point. To defuse the intellectual problem of evil you don't need to show *why* God permits certain evils and sufferings. You don't need to pinpoint the exact reasons he allowed any specific act of evil, such as the Holocaust or the death of a particular loved one. All you need to show is that it's at least *possible* for God to have reasons for permitting that evil. Because if it's even possible for him to permit the evil, then the logical problem of evil dissolves away. God may have reasons for allowing evil, even if we're not aware of them.

So, if you have a friend or family member who thinks the existence of God is logically incompatible with the existence of evil, you should ask something like, "Do you think it's at least *possible* God could have reasons for permitting pain and suffering, just as you might have reasons for allowing some pain and suffering in your life, such as visiting the dentist?" If they say yes, then you've defused their logical problem of evil. If they say no, then ask them how they can know with certainty that God could have no good reasons. The truthful answer to the question "Why did God allow this particular suffering?" is "I don't know." But because I don't know, I should take the modest position that perhaps God might have good reasons for permitting it.

THE EVIDENTIAL PROBLEM OF EVIL

With that in mind, a skeptic might claim that the amount of evidence of evil is so great, it overwhelms any reasons God may have for allowing it. To put it another way, there are so many acts of inexplicable violence and so much unjustified pain that it's extremely unlikely God exists. This differs from the logical problem of evil, which claims it's *impossible* for God to exist alongside evil. This one is less bold. This version claims only that God's existence is *extremely unlikely* given the enormous amount of evidence against him.

What kind of evidence does the skeptic have in mind? Usually evils that seem pointless or seem to serve no greater good. These might include natural evils such as hurricanes, earthquakes, and tsunamis that on the surface don't seem to be caused by humans and thus can't be solved by appealing to the greater good of free will. In those cases, we can't say, "Well, God permitted the earthquake to bring about the greater good of free will," as we could with atrocities such as murder or torture, committed directly by humans. Or we might think of seemingly pointless acts of suffering such as childhood cancer or animal suffering.

While the skeptic can't prove with certainty that such acts are pointless, they maintain that the evidence makes it highly probable the evils have no justification and therefore make it extremely unlikely God exists. So how should we answer the evidential problem of evil? My friend Trent Horn gives the best approach.[2] He suggests three methods or strategies.

The Good Reasons Approach

We have already covered a version of this strategy. This approach suggests that God permits evil and suffering because he has good reasons or because he's able to bring about a greater good. We mentioned free will above, but we can imagine many more.

In the example of natural disasters, think of the out-pouring of heroism, friendship, and solidarity that usually emerges after hurricanes or floods. After Hurricane Katrina, for instance, aid poured in from all over the world. Even Bangladesh, one of the poorest nations on earth, sent $1 million to help the relief efforts. These acts of compassion are important not only because they alleviate suffering but also because they shape the people who express them. They become better people, more virtuous, and oftentimes more faithful.

The Limited Perspective Approach

This strategy says we can guess why God might have good reasons for allowing evil, but we're not in a good position to make that assessment because our perspective is too narrow. We're restricted by space and time. We can see only a sliver of the world's events at a particular time, and no future events.

However, God can see the long-lasting and far-reaching effects of every action on earth. So, if God permits a hurricane in the Gulf of Mexico, he's immediately aware of the ripple effects of that natural disaster throughout all of space and time and throughout every human life. He can see all the damage it will produce but also see all the good that might arise. Thus, he's able to determine whether the hurricane is justified.

The skeptic who declares God likely does not have good reasons for allowing extreme suffering is on the spot. He shoulders the burden of proof. It's up to him to explain how he could possibly know that. The only way the skeptic could know whether God does or doesn't have good reasons is if he knew everything about all actions, now and into the future. But that would make him God, which he'd be reluctant to affirm, especially if he's an atheist.

So, the limited perspective approach is effective. You can simply say, "I don't know why God allowed that to happen, or whether it was justified, because I don't have the adequate perspective."

The Turning the Tables Approach

Trent Horn offers this third approach to the evidential problem. If someone suggests that God probably doesn't exist, given the enormous amount of evil in the world, instead of battling over the evidence, you can just focus on the standard of evil itself. In the first chapter on atheism, we saw why objective moral standards are only possible in light of a moral lawgiver. If you want to call something truly, objectively evil, then you need an objective moral standard. And objective morality can only be possible with God. Thus, if a skeptic contends that the vast amount of evil in the world makes God unlikely, you can respond by saying without God, there would be no such thing as evil to begin with. There would be no way to define certain events as objectively wrong. The skeptic can't have it both ways. He can't use evil to disprove God, as evil depends on an objective moral standard such as God.

Also, for this evidential problem of evil, we're weighing the evidence for and against God. But the prevalence of evil isn't the only factor. We also need to consider the multiple, strong arguments *for* God's existence, which were treated in the first chapter. Even if the problem of evil plants some doubt in our minds, or makes us question whether God really exists, the overwhelming evidence *for* God's existence can overcome those doubts and convince us that God is nevertheless real.

Those are some different ways to handle the evidential problem of evil. You probably won't want to employ all three approaches in a single conversation, but now you have multiple tools in your bag, and you can use the right one, depending on whom you're talking with.

Expert Interview with Peter Kreeft

➤ **Watch the interview here: https://claritasu.com/kreeft**

Peter Kreeft is a professor of philosophy at Boston College and the author of more than seventy-five books. One of his most popular books is titled *Making Sense Out of Suffering*, which is his response to the problem of evil and suffering.

In this interview, he responds to the following questions:

1. Why does God allow so much suffering in the world?
2. What are your thoughts on the best-selling book *Why Do Bad Things Happen to Good People?*
3. What possible greater good could come from the Holocaust or a mass shooting?
4. How is Jesus the ultimate answer to our pain and suffering?
5. What difference does Christianity make to evil in our lives?
6. How did you get through the struggle with the near death of your daughter?
7. When discussing evil and suffering with a friend, what are some things we should say and some things we should avoid?

Excerpt from the Interview

"What happened on the Cross is in one sense the worst thing that ever happened, but God used it for the very best that ever happened—namely, our own salvation. And we dare to celebrate that horrible event on a holiday that we call Good Friday!" (Peter Kreeft)

THE EMOTIONAL PROBLEM OF EVIL

For many, maybe most people, evil is not an intellectual problem that needs solving. Instead, people in pain just want help and relief in the face of great suffering.

In those cases, we don't want to parse out a logical argument about whether God could have good reasons for allowing evil. We just want to comfort the suffering loved ones in front of us. Maybe we have a spouse or child going through health difficulties. Maybe it's a friend hit with a sudden tragedy. Maybe it's the moment our heart sinks when hearing about yet another shooting or terrorist attack. It's not our minds that challenge us in these moments but our hearts. In the face of such evil and suffering, we don't ultimately want answers; we want relief.

God Suffers with Us

What's the best response to the emotional problem of evil? What should we say when talking with someone grappling with this issue? For Christians there's really only one answer to this problem—the love of Jesus Christ. Now, I don't mean that in a sappy, pietistic way. I mean it literally. The love of Jesus Christ is the best resource to help us face suffering with hope and courage instead of bitterness and despair.

This is part of what makes Christianity unique. In Christianity we find a God who willingly suffers with his people. It is not a religion where God watches disinterestedly from afar as we suffer. Instead Christianity affirms that God himself came to earth and became one of us, not just to stand by our side and teach us things, but to suffer alongside us.

In the final years of his life, Jesus, who is both God and man, experienced every cruelty and injustice you could imagine: loss of friends, mockery, lies, torture, wrongful punishment, and execution. God allowed that brutal suffering so he could say to us, "I'm with you. I know suffering. I know evil. I've been through the worst of it and have come out the other side. And I'll get you through it too. You are not alone."

That is an incredible gift, but to be fair, this insight alone doesn't *solve* the problem of evil. It doesn't make it go away. But it does make the evil easier to bear. Men and women through the centuries have found the resolve to bear their pains and persevere because they know God has suffered with them.

An Eternal Perspective

Christianity also offers an eternal perspective that relieves pain and suffering. For Christians, this life is not the final act in the play. It's only the prologue. Suppose, for example, that a child is born, delighting his new parents. Then after just a few months, they discover the child has a rare, incurable disease. After a few heartbreaking weeks, the child suddenly passes away.

For Christians, that's not the end of the story. God promises an everlasting life, if we choose it, with eternal joy and splendor in his kingdom. He also promises that in this new life he will wipe away all our tears, right all wrongs, and end all evil, pain, and suffering. This means the baby who dies early will enjoy a new life with a new body and be reunited with his parents. The innocent people killed by tsunamis or grave acts of violence will be resurrected and experience everlasting joy. And all those who commit acts of evil and who create suffering will be held responsible. Justice will ultimately prevail; evil and injustice do *not* have the last word.

So, Christianity helps to alleviate the emotional problem of evil by offering an eternal perspective. As St. Teresa of Avila said, we'll look back on our difficult time on earth as little more than a single rough night in a bad hotel.

God's Megaphone

In C. S. Lewis's book *The Problem of Pain*, he wrote, "God whispers to us in our pleasures, speaks to us in our conscience, but shouts in our pains: It is His megaphone to rouse a deaf world."[3] When things are going well, we tend to ignore God. That doesn't mean we reject him. It just means we forget how much we depend on him.

However, when we experience deep pain or suffering, we reach out to God with great desperation, crying out for his help. We beg him to heal our loved ones or to comfort us in our pain. We ramp up our prayers, and our spiritual life shifts into high gear. Sometimes God allows us to suffer because it's only through pain that we turn back to him and reopen the lines of communication. As tough as it is to bear, evil and pain often lead people back to God.

So, we have three good responses to the emotional problem of evil: the comfort of knowing God suffers with us; the healing power of an eternal perspective; and being drawn closer to God through suffering.

ANSWERING THE BEST OBJECTIONS

Now that we've covered the three forms of the problem of evil, let's examine some common objections you'll hear from skeptics and consider how to answer them.

Objection 1: "I get that God might have good reasons for permitting some evils, but there's just so much evil in the world. Why couldn't he, say, cut it in half? The Holocaust killed six million innocent Jews. Couldn't God have prevented, say, three million of those deaths?"

There are two responses to this objection. First, perhaps God has already done that! Maybe the world was on course for twice the amount of evil we currently experience, but he has *already* cut it in half. Perhaps the Holocaust was on pace to kill twelve million innocent Jews, but God reshaped history to prevent half of those deaths.

Second, when someone says there should be less evil in the world, you can simply ask, "Well, how much evil would you find acceptable? Where would you draw the line?" The problem with demanding that God override our free will to reduce pain and suffering in *some* situations is that you need a clearly drawn line in the sand. Otherwise you can ask, "OK, God prevented half the evils around us, but why not more beyond *that*? Why not cut the evil into a quarter, or an eighth, or less?" You can always get lower.

You see what we're driving at? You can naturally keep pressing until you get all the way to the bottom and say, "Well, why wouldn't God just get rid of *all* evil and suffering in the world?" But that's the objection we answered for the evidential problem of evil. God doesn't prevent *all* evil and suffering for two reasons: first, because that would compromise our free will, and it's better to have free will alongside evil than no free will and no evil; and second, because even when God allows evil, he's able to bring about a greater good.

Objection 2: "Suppose you were walking down the street and you saw someone beating an innocent person to death but did nothing. According to our laws, you would be guilty of a crime and liable to punishment. So why does

God get a free pass when he stands by and does nothing in the face of so much evil?"

This is a good objection. It asks why we don't hold God to the same moral standard as human beings. For any human to stand by and let evil take place is a grave injustice, especially when they have the power to stop it. So why is it OK for God not to stop evil? The answer is that God has a bigger perspective than we have. Since God is able to see the full scope of time and space, he knows when a particular act of evil will result in a greater good. But given our limited understanding, we can't make that judgment, so we simply follow our obligation to stop evil as best we can.

For example, consider J. R. R. Tolkien's great masterpiece, *The Lord of the Rings*, which concerns the dark lord Sauron and his plans to overtake Middle-earth. Would we ever say Tolkien is responsible for all the evils committed by Sauron? Well, in a way, yes. It's true that Tolkien caused all those evils because he was the author of the story. Since he conceived the story in advance, he already knew from page 1 all the evil that Sauron would commit.

Nevertheless, Tolkien allowed that evil to occur. He included Sauron in his story and allowed him to express his free will, even malevolently. Tolkien knew that from those evil decisions would come greater goods, such as the renewal of Middle-earth and the heroism of the hobbits and their fellowship.

That's similar to God. God is not a character within the story, like us in this world, watching as evil is committed.

He is like Tolkien, the author of the story, who does include evil but only because, with his greater perspective, he sees how such evil will lead to even greater goods.

Objection 3: "If God knew all the damage we would commit through our free will, he should never have given us free will in the first place."

The skeptic John Loftus puts it this way. "Giving us free will is like giving a razor blade to a two-year-old child,"[4] and God should never have done something so irresponsible. This is both a bad analogy and a bad objection because toddlers can't do anything good with razor blades. At best, if we're lucky, they'll simply avoid hurting themselves, but there's no possible benefit to their having razor blades.

Free will differs from this example. When people have free will, they do have the possibility of using it for good, and often do. Of course, we can abuse our free will, making bad choices that harm us and others. But most of us agree that's a risk worth taking.

In response to this objection, you also want to emphasize that free will is an objective good. In fact, as St. Augustine argued, "a creature that sins by free will is more excellent than one that does not sin but only because it has no free will."[5] That's because without free will, we would essentially be robots. Our actions would have no meaning. Since we would not choose good or evil, there would be no such thing as praise or blame. We would have no saints and no heroes because people who acted heroically would just be doing what their preprogrammed bodies forced them to do.

They wouldn't display any real courage, bravery, sacrifice, or goodness. And notably, there would be no love, since love is a free act of the will.

So, most of us agree that free will is a valuable gift, even if we tend to abuse it sometimes. And that's why, even though God knew we would abuse it, he still chose to give us that gift.

TALKING POINTS AND TIPS

To close this chapter, here are some talking points you'll find helpful when engaging someone in a conversation about evil and suffering.

Tip 1: Don't punt to mystery.

This is another bit of advice from my friend Trent Horn. You've probably seen this happen. Someone confronts a Christian about why God allowed a particular evil to occur, maybe a deadly tsunami or a violent school shooting, and the Christian just throws up their hands and says, "Well, God just works in mysterious ways!"

Now, there's a partial truth here. It's true that God's nature is ultimately mysterious. We can't just figure out how God works by using our reason alone. We need God to reveal it to us. And given our finite intellect, even after God reveals himself to us, we can't fully understand his infinite nature.

However, punting to mystery is woefully inadequate for most people. It shortchanges them, and they deserve a more rigorous explanation, which this chapter aimed to help you do. Instead of punting to mystery, you are now prepared to say, "Well, obviously we can't know God's intentions for sure, since our perspective is so limited. But I do know that sometimes God permits certain evils in order to bring about greater goods, just as we do in our own lives. Let's think about this for a second: What goods could possibly come out of this atrocity?" Then you could suggest free will, heroic sacrifice, selfless love, or other possibilities. That will get the conversation moving in a better direction.

Tip 2: Don't try to solve the problem of evil.

This is the reverse of the first tip. You don't want to punt to mystery, but you also don't want the other extreme that pretends you're absolutely sure why God permitted a certain evil. Ultimately, the problem of evil is not one that can be tied up with a nice, neat bow and solved forever. It's too complicated and neuralgic, especially for people who have suffered deeply.

So, you should not aim to solve the problem. Instead, you should seek at least to prevent it from being a stumbling block for people on the road toward God. You likely won't get people to the point where they'll say, "Aha! That makes complete sense! Now I'll never struggle with evil again!" But you can get them to the point where they think, "OK, I still don't understand most of the evil around me, but I no longer think that's a good reason to doubt God's existence or his love. I see how the two might fit together."

Tip 3: Determine which subissue is most pressing.

Since each problem of evil—the logical, evidential, and emotional—requires a different strategy, you want to determine which one the person you're talking with has the most difficulty with. You may determine this by saying something like, "I know you have a hard time believing in God because of all the evil and suffering you've experienced. But let me ask you, is this more of an intellectual problem for you, or more of a personal or emotional issue? In other words, is this more of a philosophical problem you have, as in you don't think evil and God could logically coexist? Or is this more of an emotional problem where you're grasping for help and relief?" Their response to that should give you a better sense of which strategies will be most effective.

I mentioned in the last tip that you shouldn't try to solve the whole problem of evil. Generally, that's true. However, I do think the *logical* problem can be solved with certainty. You can show people, as we did above (see pp. 36–38), how there is no logical contradiction between an all-good, all-powerful God and the existence of evil. So that subissue can, in fact, be solved.

The evidential problem can't be solved in the same way, but it's possible to help people see the likelihood of God allowing certain evils to exist, in order to bring about greater goods.

However, the emotional problem really can't be solved *at all*. Yet still, Christianity offers help: the accompaniment of the crucified and resurrected Christ, who strengthens us to endure any evil.

So, don't try to solve the whole problem of evil, with all three versions. You can't do it. But you *can* help people solve the logical problem, make sense of the evidential problem, and find comfort despite the emotional problem.

RECOMMENDED BOOKS
(in order of importance)

Peter Kreeft, *Making Sense Out of Suffering* (Servant Books, 1986).

> Kreeft dismisses easy answers that try to explain evil away, showing why they ultimately fail. Then he turns to philosophers, artists, and prophets looking for "clues" to the meaning of pain and suffering. Finally, he turns to Jesus, explaining what difference Christianity makes in responding to the problem of evil.

C. S. Lewis, *The Problem of Pain* (HarperOne, 2015).

> Lewis wrestles with the problem of why we suffer. Of special interest is his handling of common misunderstandings of the qualities of God that are often under assault when evil arises: his being all-good or all-powerful. He includes a unique chapter on animal pain.

Alvin Plantinga, *God, Freedom, and Evil* (Eerdmans, 1989).

> Plantinga definitively puts the logical problem of evil to rest by demonstrating that there is no contradiction

between an all-loving, all-powerful God and the existence of evil.

Paul Murray, O.P., *Scars: Essays, Poems, and Meditations on Affliction* (Bloomsbury Continuum, 2014).

Fr. Murray doesn't try to explain the existence of evil. Instead, he tells stories of people who have suffered intensely and yet found meaning and serenity amid their pain. He closes the book with a beautiful meditation on Jesus' last words from the Cross.

David Bentley Hart, *The Doors of the Sea: Where Was God in the Tsunami?* (Eerdmans, 2005).

In response to the horrific December 2004 tsunami in Asia that claimed roughly 250,000 lives, Hart gives consoling answers to the problem of natural evils like earthquakes, cancer, and sudden death.

FOR REFLECTION AND DISCUSSION

1. In your own words, explain why the problem of evil is the best objection to God and Christianity.
2. How does the emotional problem of evil differ from the logical and evidential problems?
3. What can you say to a person who believes there is a contradiction between an all-powerful God and the existence of evil?

4. How would you respond to a person who claims there's so much evidence for evil in the world that it's likely God does not exist?
5. What does Christianity offer to someone who is experiencing great personal suffering or pain?

FOR PRACTICE

For each of the following scenarios, write a response using what you learned in this chapter.

1. A skeptical friend objects, "Anyone who walks into a children's hospital knows there is no God. Or at the very least, they know God can't be all-good. No all-good God would allow the suffering and pain these children experience on a daily basis."
2. An astute atheist makes the following objection: "You say it's good that we have free will. But couldn't God have given us free will and put us all in heaven right now? Or do you deny those in heaven have free will? It seems to me you are stuck in a dilemma: (1) Those in heaven don't have free will, yet they are better off than us, so it would be better for us not to have free will, or (2) those in heaven have free will yet without any evil being present, so God could have made our world like that too. What do you say to that?"

3

TRUSTING THE GOSPELS

THREE KEY PRINCIPLES

The other day I was listening to a debate between a Christian and an atheist. The two men were discussing Jesus' early apostles, and specifically whether the apostles were martyred for their faith. The Christian took the traditional position that all of them were killed for their beliefs, except St. John, who was boiled alive but somehow survived.

The discussion started off cordial and interesting, but partway into the interview, as the Christian began talking about the apostles, the atheist interrupted to say, "Well, hold on a minute. That's all quite interesting, but you're assuming the apostles actually existed . . ."

"Huh?" the Christian replied, "What do you mean? You don't think the apostles existed?" The atheist immediately said, "No, the only evidence we have is the Bible, which is a holy book filled with obvious bias. I don't accept it; it's not a reliable text. The authors were more interested in theology than history. Show me something outside the Bible, some early century, nonbiblical text that talks about the apostles, and maybe I'll take them seriously."

Now, let's pause for a moment. Put yourself in that position. What would *you* say if you were in the Christian's shoes? You're talking with someone when you realize they not only doubt whether the apostles died for their faith but also doubt the apostles *even existed*, and they're skeptical about the Bible in general. What would you say?

Well, if you're not sure, that's OK. That's why you're holding this book! We'll come back to this specific challenge about the apostles in a moment, but it offers a springboard for this chapter. Here we're concerned with one main question: Can we trust the Bible? Does the Bible, and specifically the gospels, contain reliable history? Do we have good reasons to trust what the gospels say about Jesus and his followers?

These were precisely the questions where the Christian and atheist disagreed. On the one hand, the Christian trusted the gospel accounts. On the other hand, the atheist didn't. So, they needed to settle that question before moving on. And so do we! We want to speak clearly and confidently about the trustworthiness of the gospels, and three core principles will help establish this:

1. The Gospels Record Real Historical Events

Don't let people try to tell you the gospels are simply myths, legends, fairy tales, or helpful spiritual stories. No, the gospels are historically accurate texts that record what really happened two thousand years ago in ancient Israel, to a man named Jesus of Nazareth and the friends and enemies around him. This is very important. Once you understand that the gospel writers were intending to capture historical truth, it's much easier to trust them.

2. Treat the Gospels Like Other Historical Texts

Second, when demonstrating that the gospels are trustworthy, we should treat them as any other historical text. This is what the Christian should have said to the atheist in the interview: "OK, you don't believe the gospels are inspired by God, or are holy in the religious sense. That's fine. I get that. But then let's treat them like any other ancient document and judge them by the same criteria. Suppose an archaeologist dug up these four texts in a long, lost city—Matthew, Mark, Luke, and John—and dated them to the first or second century. Then let's examine what they have to say, using all of our best textual analysis, to try to figure out whether they're historically accurate." So, let's treat the gospels as we would any ancient historical text, judging them by the same criteria.

3. Do Not Assume the Gospels Are Inspired and Free of Error

In the context of this chapter, we're *not* assuming the gospels are inspired by God and free from error. In other words, we are *not* concerned about biblical inspiration. We Christians, of course, are convinced that the whole Bible *is* inspired and free from error. We believe every verse has God as its author or, to use the language of the *Catechism of the Catholic Church*, that the Bible is the Word of God written in the words of men.[1] However, as we simply want to know whether we can trust the gospels as historical documents, we're *not* trying to prove that they are inspired or inerrant. So, we'll bracket those questions for now and will just treat these texts as any other ancient historical document. In fact, if it helps in a discussion with a skeptic, you can even assume, for the sake of argument, that the gospels are *not* inspired and that they *do* contain errors. But even if that were true, those are not reasons to dismiss the gospels wholesale. Every other ancient document contains errors, and it's the historian's job to separate fact from error.

Again, our aim here is to examine the gospels just as historians examine other ancient documents such as Plutarch's *Lives*, the historical writings of Josephus, or the ancient epics by Homer. We'll use the same criteria we use for those other writings, judging the gospels to see whether they offer reliable historical accounts.

Getting clear on those three points will help us avoid a lot of pitfalls. For instance, let's return to that discussion between the Christian and the atheist. The atheist dismissed the gospels because they were written by biased authors, men with a religious agenda. That may be true, but that's the case with every historical document. Every author has a purpose, or an agenda. That's no reason to dismiss the texts, and it's therefore no reason to dismiss the gospels. Let's treat the gospels fairly as any other ancient document.

What about the atheist's demand for other nonbiblical accounts of the apostles from the first or second century? Well, we do have early, outside writings that confirm much of Christianity, including several first-century references to the life and death of Jesus. But simply dismissing the gospels themselves rejects the *earliest* and *best* evidence we have. In fact, the four traditional gospels—Matthew, Mark, Luke, and John—were included in the Bible (despite other so-called gospels being left out) because they were regarded as the *most accurate* and *reliable*. In other words, the fact that the earliest Christians lifted these four accounts above others, because of their truthfulness, is a check in their favor, not against them. We shouldn't dismiss these four texts, out of the gate, simply because they've been collected in a book that Christians hold sacred. That would be irresponsible and unfair. Scholars never react that way to other historical documents.

But let's explore some of the main reasons people doubt the Bible. We've already seen one example with our atheist debater, but what are some other reasons people don't believe what the gospels say about Jesus?

WHY DO PEOPLE DOUBT THE GOSPELS?

I was in college when my faith started to bloom. I was at Florida State University, studying mechanical engineering, and although I was already into my engineering and science courses, I figured I wanted to take at least one religion class while in school. So, in my senior year, I signed up for Introduction to the New Testament. I figured, "Hey, this will be great! I'll get to study the Bible, read books about Jesus, and I'll earn college credit for doing it!"

But I learned quickly that's not how things would go. At the beginning of the very first class, before even going over the syllabus, the professor went around the room and asked each person to "describe their experience with the New Testament." As expected, some students said they knew a little about the Bible but had never read it personally. Many were Catholic, Baptist, or some form of Christian and shared how they loved the Bible and tried to study it every day.

But after everyone was done sharing, the teacher said she wanted to make it quite clear this class was not a Bible study. It would not be about stirring your faith, or generating warm devotional feelings, or helping you grow closer to Jesus. This class would not even be taught from a Christian perspective. The teacher's goal was about one thing—"uncovering the truth about the Bible." The implication seemed to be that whatever it is you think you know about the Bible, you're probably wrong. Then the teacher explained that most people are completely unaware that the Bible contains many errors, that it was poorly copied over hundreds of years, and that we don't even know who wrote most of the New Testament. This means, she said, that most of the sayings and miracles attributed to Jesus probably didn't happen and were fabricated much later, long after Jesus died.

I looked around the room. Most of the students were stunned. And if that wasn't enough, the teacher said all this with sort of a half smile, clearly delighting in undermining the faith of so many young people.

But that wasn't the end of it. The teacher announced that our text for the class would be *Introduction to the New*

Testament, a popular book written by Bart Ehrman. I didn't know who he was at the time, but I later discovered that Ehrman, while admittedly a world-class Bible scholar, is widely regarded as America's most prominent biblical skeptic. He's an aggressive agnostic who has written several best-selling books casting doubt on Jesus and the Bible. Perhaps his two most famous books are *Misquoting Jesus: The Story behind Who Changed the Bible and Why* and *How Jesus Became God: The Exaltation of a Jewish Preacher from Galilee.*

So when I thought I was signing up for a course that would encourage my faith, I ended up with a New Testament class taught by an agnostic professor with a textbook written by a notorious Bible skeptic. Many of my classmates finished the year unsure whether they could trust the Bible or believe anything it says about Jesus.

Unfortunately, this is an all-too-common story. Many kids go off to college and meet skeptical professors or classmates for the first time and then come home with their faith ripped to shreds. Others meet friends or coworkers who think the Bible is some fanciful, made-up book that is on par with *Grimm's Fairy Tales* or *Aesop's Fables.*

This doesn't happen by accident. Over the last century, prominent doubters have ruthlessly questioned scripture. For example, there are the scholars who make up the so-called Jesus Seminar, a traveling colloquium spearheaded by John Dominic Crossan and the late Marcus Borg. These scholars aim to discover the "historical Jesus" or the "Jesus of history," which they distinguish from the "Christ of faith." They suggest that the Jesus religious people worship in their churches probably includes a mix of legendary and mythical accretions. This is a common tactic today, to attempt a split between the "Jesus of history" and the "Christ of faith." But as we'll come to see, there aren't really two different Jesuses. That's a false dichotomy. As Pope Benedict XVI has written, there's only one Jesus: the "Jesus of history" *is* the "Christ of faith."

In addition to the Jesus Seminar skeptics, we have the New Atheists. We met some of them in the first chapter. Few of these atheists are legitimate Bible scholars, but they nevertheless try to cast doubt on the Bible in order to cast doubt on God. Their typical move is to claim the Bible is full of injustice, absurdity, cruelty, violence, and intolerance, and therefore has no authority and shouldn't be trusted. In fact, one atheist even published a *Skeptic's Annotated Bible*, which surrounds the biblical text with notes commenting on all of its supposed errors, contradictions, and discrepancies.

So, from Bart Ehrman to the Jesus Seminar to the New Atheists, many people are doubting the Bible today, including the New Testament where we learn most of what we know about Jesus.

Let's dig a little deeper into these objections and look at five specific reasons people doubt the gospels.

Dating

First, many skeptics think the New Testament texts were written long after the events they describe, whether that be several decades or even centuries. They assume Jesus died around AD 30 but that the four gospels weren't recorded until several decades or maybe even a century after that. And if that's the case, how can we be sure they weren't distorted and manipulated over time?

Authorship

A second objection has to do with authorship. Some skeptics, such as Bart Ehrman, claim that we don't know who wrote the original gospel manuscripts, since not all of them say, "The Gospel according to Mark" as our modern Bibles do. And if we don't know who wrote them, we can't be sure the texts are reliable.

Bias

A third objection appeals to bias. Some skeptics dismiss the gospel accounts simply because they were written by Christians who had an obvious bias and thus can't be trusted. Doubters claim they would believe these stories if they were written by an unbiased source, maybe a non-Christian historian from the first century. But since the Christians were obviously motivated to get people to join their religion, skeptics claim we can't take their writings seriously.

Errors and Contradictions

A fourth objection deals with apparent errors and contradictions. This objection comes from seeing conflicts in the gospels. These range from different chronologies for the same events to differing accounts such as whether Mary Magdalene was alone or with other women at Jesus' tomb. The skeptic claims there is not just one or two apparent contradictions but hundreds or even thousands. And if the gospels contain that many errors, there's no way we can trust them.

Miracles

A fifth and final objection has to do with miracles. Most don't think the gospels are reliable simply because they contain miracles. Their logic runs something like this: (1) We know people can't perform miracles; (2) the gospels describe miracles; and (3) therefore, the gospels must be unreliable.

These are the five main reasons skeptics doubt the gospels, and most of their criticisms fall within one of those five categories. Just to recap: first, the dating (the gospels were written too late); second, the authorship (we don't know who wrote the gospels); third, the purported bias (they were all written by Christians with an agenda); fourth, the apparent errors and contradictions (hundreds of thousands of discrepancies); and fifth, the miracles.

Now, to get you clear and confident about discussing the Bible, we're going to handle each of these objections. Let's begin by tackling the first two together.

WHO REALLY WROTE THE GOSPELS?

If we want to show that the gospels are trustworthy, we need to show that they are *authentic*, *pure*, and *reliable*. Those three qualities together make a text trustworthy.

Authentic. First, the gospels must have been written by the people who claim to have written them, and at an early date. If some forger wrote them in the third or fourth century, then they aren't authentic. They're fakes. But if they were written by disciples of Jesus, or people who knew the original disciples during the lifetime of eyewitnesses, then we can be confident they're authentic.

Pure. Second, we must show that the gospels are pure. Did the gospel texts change over time? How do we know the gospel accounts we read today are the same accounts that were originally written almost two thousand years ago? Maybe the originals were authentic, but the copies aren't accurate. Perhaps the texts got mangled over time. We need to show not only that the texts were originally genuine but that we can trust the copied versions we have today.

Reliable. Finally, after showing the gospels to be authentic and pure, what about the content itself? Are the stories and sayings in the gospels reliable? Maybe the original gospels were not forgeries, and our copies today match the originals, but what if the writers just originally made everything up? What if they just wanted to get attention or start a new religion? How do we know they were recording actual history and not just inventing myths?

So, let's start with that first criterion, authenticity. Of course, today we refer to the gospels as "the Gospel according to Matthew/Mark/Luke/John." But were those really the people who wrote them?

People are usually surprised to learn that many biblical scholars believe the gospels were anonymous. They claim the original versions of the gospels did not carry any titles. And if the gospels were originally anonymous, it's reasonable to conclude that none of them were written by an eyewitness or even by someone who knew an eyewitness. The accounts would be second- or third- or fourth-hand stories at best, and thus far less reliable.

The same scholars typically believe that the gospels circulated for almost a century without titles, before anyone attributed them to Matthew, Mark, Luke, or John. It was only then, much later, long after Jesus' disciples were dead and buried, that the titles we have today were finally added to the manuscripts.

But is this "anonymous gospel" theory true? Interestingly, many scholars are beginning to doubt this theory. And there are a few reasons. First, despite its popularity, the theory's biggest weakness is that there is zero evidence to support it. We have no anonymous copies of Matthew, Mark, Luke, or John. None have ever been found. Every gospel manuscript we have bears a title or heading. We have absolutely no evidence of an anonymous gospel, which means the theory is purely speculative.

A second major problem is that every single one of the ancient manuscripts we do have—not some, but *all*, without exception, and in every language—attribute each gospel to either Matthew, Mark, Luke, or John. In other words, they're not only not anonymous but also actually attributed to the people we traditionally attribute them to.

A third problem is the implausibility of an anonymous document circulating around the Roman Empire without a title for almost a hundred years, and then suddenly scribes, all around the world, attributing each copy of the text to exactly the same author with no trace of disagreement. If the "anonymous gospel" theory were true, we would expect the same gospel to be assigned to different authors in various places. But this never happened. Throughout history, each of the gospels has been assigned to one, and only one, author. In each case, it's the author we know today—Matthew, Mark, Luke, or John.

Finally, the writings of the early Church Fathers provide external evidence of the true authorship. These were ancient Christian leaders who lived in the first few centuries after Christ, and their writings agree about who wrote the four gospels. For example, Papias (in AD 130) and Irenaeus (in AD 180) both confirm that Matthew wrote the gospel assigned to him. Clement of Alexandria (writing in AD 200) joined the same two early Church Fathers in confirming that Mark wrote the gospel assigned to him. We find similar confirmations for Luke and John. Our earliest historical records outside the Bible unanimously testify that Matthew, Mark, Luke, and John wrote these gospels.

But who were these men? Without getting into all the details, we actually know about each figure both from the Bible and from early historians and the Church Fathers. Matthew and John were both apostles of Jesus, men who lived and journeyed with Jesus 24/7 for about three years. They were direct eyewitnesses to everything he said and did. Mark was a follower and translator of the apostle Peter. He never met Jesus personally, but he knew several eyewitnesses who did, and his gospel is based on the testimony of Peter. Similarly, Luke was a second-generation

Christian who was a follower of the apostle Paul and also a well-known physician to the early Christian community. He based his gospel on the testimony and preaching of Paul.

In summary, people who personally knew Jesus or who recorded the testimony of those who did wrote all four gospels. The gospels are not later hand-me-down stories. They're based on direct eyewitness testimony. And since that's the case, and since we know who wrote them, they are authentic.

But when were the gospels written? Was it centuries after the events they record? Today, most scholars think Matthew, Mark, and Luke were written in the seventies, eighties, or nineties. But a strong case can be made that they were written in the early sixties within just a few decades of Jesus' death. And the Gospel of John is widely supposed to have been written around AD 90–95, shortly before he died in AD 98.

That means that apostles, or close followers of the apostles, wrote all four gospels during the living memory of these witnesses—which is important, because living witnesses would have challenged any inaccurate accounts. So we have good reason to think the gospels contain early, eyewitness testimony, and thus good reason to trust them.

But being authentic is one thing. How do we know that later copyists didn't take these authentic gospels and then distort them over time?

DID THE GOSPELS CHANGE OVER TIME?

Most of us remember, as kids, playing the Telephone Game. Here's how it works. A group of children sit in a circle. And then one child comes up with a message, something like, "I ate chocolate on Easter." That child then whispers the message into the ear of the next child, who whispers it to the next child, and so on, all the way around the circle. By the time the last child shares the message out loud, it's usually some wildly hilarious distortion far different than the original version. So, the message "I ate chocolate on Easter" suddenly becomes "I hate chalk and my feet hurt."

I remember playing the Telephone Game as a child, but I never thought about it again until college. As I sat in my Introduction to the New Testament course, the one taught by the agnostic professor, I once again heard about the Telephone Game. But this time, it was in regard to the Bible. My teacher suggested the gospels were the products of a sort of historical Telephone Game. According to her—and she's far from the only scholar who believes this—the stories about Jesus were passed down from person to person, over hundreds of years and across thousands of miles, until they were eventually recorded in the gospels. Then from there they were copied from book to book, monk by monk, until finally the texts came down to us two thousand years later. Imagine, critics suggest, if we so mangle a message in the Telephone Game, how badly the gospel message must have been distorted! If a dozen kids sitting in a circle can't even pass along a single sentence accurately, how can we expect hundreds of people over thousands of years to accurately pass down four books containing tens of thousands of words? Isn't it likely these stories became warped over time? These are good questions.

First, let's briefly respond to the Telephone Game analogy. The main problem with this comparison is that the whole purpose of the Telephone Game is to come up with a jumbled version of the original message. That's what makes it fun. If the original message makes its way around the room and is repeated exactly the same at the end, then the game is considered a failure. Nobody is happy; nobody wants that. That's why some people *purposely* distort the message before whispering it to the next person.

But the transmission of the gospels was far different. The Christians who passed down this information were deeply concerned about accuracy. Their goal was to transmit it as correctly as possible, as they considered each word spoken by or about Jesus to be sacred, like pearls on a string, and they treated them with that sort of reverence. When they shared these words, or copied them in print, they considered it a sacred duty to do so accurately, since passing on these words was a matter of salvation. So, for all those reasons, the Telephone Game is just not a good analogy.

But we have other reasons to trust the gospels are pure. One powerful example is the manuscript evidence. When you open your Bible today, you'll see on the copyright page that your translation was published sometime within the last few years and in an English translation. But the original gospels were written in a different language, either Hebrew or Greek, around two thousand years ago. So how do we know our texts from today match the original versions?

Scholars answer this question by comparing modern texts to the earliest available ones. Ideally, we'd want to compare our modern texts to the *original* manuscripts. But sadly, we don't have any original gospel texts or what textual experts call "autographs." The autographs for each gospel were likely written on cheap materials that deteriorated quickly. They just didn't survive. But copies of these texts were made almost immediately on more sturdy materials, in order to circulate them widely to churches across the land. Thankfully, we have access to many of those early copies. And even better, because we have so many copies, we can compare them to each other to build a strong idea about what the original texts said.

What's remarkable is how many we have. We have more early copies of the gospels than any other text in the ancient world. When I first discovered this fact, I was amazed. Scholars are aware of more than 5,300 ancient manuscripts that contain some portion of the New Testament, and that total is still growing. Our earliest manuscripts are dated around AD 125, which puts them just a few decades away from the original texts.

Now, a few decades may still sound like a long period of time, but keep two things in mind. First, that means our earliest copies were still produced within the living memory of Jesus' disciples and witnesses. Those early copies could not have been falsified or distorted without witnesses repudiating any such tampering with the gospels. People were still alive who saw and heard these events.

Second, that gap of a few decades between the original manuscript and our earliest copy is by far the smallest gap between the originals and copies of any ancient text. For comparison, the gap between the original text of Homer's *Iliad* and our earliest copy of the *Iliad* is around four hundred years, and that's considered a relatively small gap. For the writings of Plato, the gap between his original texts and our first copy is more than 1,300 years! Also, we have about two hundred ancient copies of Plato and 1,700 ancient copies of *The Iliad*, but as we noted, we have more than 5,300 manuscripts that carry texts from the New Testament.

To sum up, no ancient document is better attested by multiple, early manuscripts than the New Testament. It's not even close. So if a skeptic is going to doubt the textual accuracy of the gospels, then to be consistent, he must also doubt the textual accuracy *of every other ancient document* since the gospels have the strongest manuscript evidence around.

This is why we stressed earlier how important it is to encourage skeptics to judge the gospels just as any other ancient text. Because when we do, the gospels shine far brighter by almost every historical metric.

But what about those early manuscripts? Do they match what is in our Bibles today? Bart Ehrman doesn't think so. The skeptical scholar says in his book *Misquoting Jesus* that there are thousands upon thousands of variations, so many, he says, that "there are more differences among our manuscripts than there are words in the New Testament."[2] How can that be? Well, consider that if we have 5,700 manuscripts, that means conservatively there must have been at least 20,000 copies floating around, most of which were lost to time. But if each copy had only five variations—a misspelling here, a different word there—suddenly you have 100,000 variations, which sounds like a lot until you realize you only have five variations in each manuscript.

Also, the overwhelming majority of these variants are minor, such as changing the order of words—for example, "Jesus Christ" to "Christ Jesus"—or insignificant adjustments, such as "I thank God always for you" versus "I thank *my* God always for you." In fact, biblical scholar Craig Blomberg says that "only about a tenth of one percent [of the variations] are interesting enough to make their way into footnotes of most English translations [of the Bible]. But it cannot be emphasized strongly enough that no orthodox doctrine or ethical practice of Christianity depends solely on any disputed wording."[3]

None of these variations affect any core teaching about Jesus or Christianity. Interestingly, Bart Ehrman even concedes this point. Despite slamming the Bible for its thousands of variations, in the appendix to his book *Misquoting Jesus*—located in the back of the book, where few readers will turn—he admits that "essential Christian beliefs are not affected by textual variants in the manuscript tradition of the New Testament."[4] Too bad he didn't say that on the dustjacket of his book!

In the end, the overwhelming quantity and unparalleled quality of the New Testament manuscripts confirm that if any historical text has been accurately passed down to us, it must be the gospels. The gospels are not just authentic; they are also pure, and we can have a high degree of confidence about that.

But what about that last question: They might be authentic and pure, but are the gospels reliable? Maybe our Bibles today substantially match the original manuscripts, but how do we know those original manuscripts contained real history and not just made-up stories?

LEGEND OR HISTORY?

Perhaps Jesus' early disciples just made up stories about him, so that even if people faithfully copied and passed those stories down over time, the original accounts were suspect. So how do we determine whether this happened?

Our first task is to determine the genre of the texts. We need to know what kind of books the gospels were. Were they intended to present a biography of Jesus? A history? Something fictional, like a novel? Perhaps a myth, a legend, or a fairy tale?

Even though many skeptics would answer "myth" or "fairy tale," we have good reasons to think the genre of the gospels is what we might call "ancient biography." When you look at biographies from the ancient world, including those by Josephus, Plutarch, Seutonius, and Lucian, you find five distinct traits that identify these books in the genre of "ancient biography." And the gospels share all five traits. Brant Pitre lists these in his book *The Case for Jesus*, and I'll adapt them here.[5]

1. One Person

First, ancient biographies focus on the life and death of a single individual. Other kinds of writing, such as history, focus on much wider events of an entire nation or people. But ancient biographies center on just one person. And that's what we find in the gospels. They're primarily interested in the life of one person, Jesus of Nazareth.

2. Short Length

Second, ancient biographies typically average between ten and twenty thousand words. In our own day, that's equivalent to a short book of about forty to eighty pages. They tended to be longer than letters but shorter than histories. All four gospels fit this mold. The shortest gospel is Mark at eleven thousand words, and the longest gospel is Luke at nineteen thousand words.

3. Ancestry

Third, ancient biographies often begin with ancestry. This is the first clue that the book you're reading belongs to the biography genre and not myth or legend. When a story begins with "Once upon a time . . . ," you know it's a fairy tale. If it begins, "Paul . . . to all God's beloved in Rome . . . ," then you know you're reading a letter. But if it begins with a genealogy of real, historical people, such as "Jesus, the son of Joseph, the son of Heli, the son of Matthat, and so on," then you're clued in that this is ancient biography. Not every biography begins this way, and it's true that not every gospel does either, but if it does, you have another confirmation of the genre. And two of our gospels start with this sort of ancestry.

4. No Chronological Order

Fourth, ancient biographies don't have to be in chronological order. This is important to understand. Many skeptics dismiss the gospels because they don't present history the way we present it today—namely, in strictly chronological accounts of a person's life: first his birth, then event A, followed by event B, followed by event C, and so on until his death. But ancient biographers were far more interested in arranging the material topically or thematically. For example, listen to what the Roman biographer, Seutonius, says in his life of Caesar Augustus, written in the second century. He writes: "Having given as it were a summary of his life, I shall now take up its various phases one by one, not in chronological order, but by categories, to make the account clearer and more intelligible."[6]

Modern biographers are far more interested in exactitude, noting the precise date, time, and place each event happened. But ancient authors cared more about the meaning and message of the biographical stories, and this is precisely what we find in the gospels. Sometimes the events are out of order, but that doesn't make them folklore or fiction. It just means the writers had a different purpose than do modern biographers.

5. Not in Detail

Finally, ancient biographies don't tell you everything about
a person. Listen to what Plutarch says in his biography of
Alexander the Great, written in the second century: "It is
the life of Alexander the king, and of Caesar, who overthrew
Pompey, that I am writing in this book, and the multitude
of deeds to be treated is so great that I shall make no other
preface than to entreat my readers, in case I do not tell of
all the famous actions of these men, nor even speak exhaus-
tively at all in each particular case, but in epitome for the
most part, not to complain. For it is not Histories I am writing, but Lives."[7]

In other words, Plutarch was writing not a history of
the Greek empire but a "life" of Alexander the Great. Does
that make his biography unhistorical? Of course not. It just
makes it incomplete. The same is true of the gospels. They
were not written to tell us everything Jesus said and did,
or everything about first-century Israel. In fact, the Gospel
of John explicitly says, in its closing words, "There are also
many other things which Jesus did; were every one of them
to be written, I suppose that the world itself could not contain the books that would be written" (Jn 21:25).

That's almost exactly what Plutarch said in his biography of Alexander the Great, and nobody doubts *that* biography is generally reliable. Could John be any clearer that he
is writing the same type of biography? As Pitre concludes,
"The old idea that the gospels are not biographies but folklore and fairy stories completely fails to reckon with the

literary evidence. It is long since time for it to be consigned
to the trash bin of history. The gospels are biographies."[8]

But the fact that the gospels fit the genre of ancient biography only takes us partway there. How do we know
the accounts are accurate, that they contain reliable history? Let's briefly look at a few reasons to think they're
trustworthy.

1. Writers' Intent

First, the writers themselves claim that they intended to
give an accurate account. Luke begins his gospel by saying,
"Since many have undertaken to compile a narrative of the
events that have been fulfilled among us, just as those who
were eyewitnesses from the beginning and ministers of the
word have handed them down to us, I too have decided,
after investigating everything accurately anew, to write it
down in an orderly sequence for you, most excellent The-
ophilus, *so that you may realize the certainty* of the teachings
you have received" (Lk 1:1–4, emphasis added). Luke says
that he has talked to multiple witnesses and has gathered
all of their testimony to produce an accurate historical summary of the facts.

2. Multiple, Independent Sources

Second, the gospels are reliable because they depend on
multiple, independent sources for their stories. Historians are typically happy if they can find two independent
sources for an ancient event. But with the gospels, we have
not one or two sources but *four* sources, which even though

they share some material, are substantially independent and rely on several other unique sources such as the testimonies of Mary, Peter, Paul, and other disciples of Jesus. In other words, we have more independent sources for the life of Jesus than virtually any other ancient figure.

3. The Criterion of Embarrassment

Third, to determine whether a text is reliable, historians often use something called the "criterion of embarrassment." To put it simply, if an account contains material that is embarrassing to its author or subject, that's a sign the author did not make it up. After all, if you were going to make up a story, you would make the subject and author appear as attractive and respectable as possible. But that's not what we find in the gospels. They routinely depict the disciples, the very people who wrote the gospels or supplied the testimony, as misguided, weak, and cowardly. Similarly, the gospels even make the main hero of the story, Jesus, appear sorrowful in the Garden of Gethsemane, despairing on the Cross, and ignorant when he didn't know the day and time of his Second Coming. Ancient mythmakers would never present their heroes that way.

4. Nonmythical Style

Finally, as the great literary scholar C. S. Lewis points out, if you're actually familiar with ancient myths and legends, you'll see the gospels just don't have the same texture and style—they don't *sound* like mythical stories. For example, ancient myths typically don't contain small, irrelevant details the way our modern novels do. In a modern novel, you might read about what a man ate for breakfast, or how he ironed his shirt before leaving the house. Ancient legends didn't include little details like that. However, we do find such details throughout the gospel accounts. For example, before speaking to the woman caught in adultery, there's a brief description of Jesus writing in the sand. Why was that included? It has no obvious purpose. The only reason it was included, Lewis says, is because it actually happened. That just happened to be what Jesus was doing at the moment, and the writers, wanting to be as accurate as possible, included it.

Let's pause now and recap the main points that demonstrate the trustworthiness of the gospels. We affirmed that we should examine the gospels just as we would any other ancient text. When we do, we find they fit into the category of ancient biography. And these ancient biographies seem to be true accounts of what really happened, not just fabricated myths or legends.

Expert Interview with Brant Pitre

➤ **Watch the interview here: https://claritasu.com/pitre**

Dr. Brant Pitre is distinguished research professor of scripture at the Augustine Institute. He received his PhD in New Testament and ancient Judaism from the University of Notre Dame. Pitre is author of several best-selling books, including *The Case for Jesus* (Image, 2016).

In this interview, Pitre responds to the following questions:

1. How do we know the gospels are true? What genre are they? When were they written?
2. Who wrote the gospels? Were they written by people who followed and knew Jesus directly or by people further down the line? What do you say about the "anonymous gospel" theory? Were the gospels really anonymous, or did they have names attached to them?
3. How do we know that the information passed down through the decades is true? How does it not get garbled like messages in the Telephone Game?
4. What is meant by the external and internal evidence of reliability in the gospels themselves?
5. How do you respond to the charge that the Bible is merely myth and legend?

Excerpt from the Interview

"I would just say to the atheist, you need to go back and read a few more myths if you think that when you read the gospels you've seen a myth, because you obviously don't know one when you see one." (Brant Pitre)

ANSWERING THE BEST BIBLE CRITICS

Now we have good reasons to trust the gospels. So, let's consider six of the best objections to the gospels and how to respond to them. Remember, the key to clarity is threefold: you need to be clear about what you believe, clear about the best objections to your beliefs, and clear about how to answer them. It's that last task we're focusing on here.

Objection 1: "The gospels were anonymous. Since we don't even know who wrote them, how can we trust them?"

The short response is that the gospels were not anonymous. Every single one of the earliest manuscripts we have attributes the text to Matthew, Mark, Luke, or John. We don't have a single early manuscript without a title. The "anonymous gospel" theory is popular today but totally baseless. If someone proposes this objection, simply reply, "Why do you think the gospels were anonymous? What evidence do you have?" They won't be able to supply any, because there isn't any.

Objection 2: "The gospels were recorded long after the events happened–probably several decades, or perhaps a century. That's just too big of a gap for them to be accurate!"

In response we can say that scholars think Matthew, Mark, and Luke were written in the seventies or eighties, but a strong case can be made that they were written in the early sixties, within just a few decades of Jesus' death. And the Gospel of John is widely supposed to have been written around AD 90–95. At most, we're talking about forty to seventy years between the actual events and the writing of the gospels. Now, that may seem like a lot of time, but we should keep three things in mind.

First, ancient Jews had extraordinary memories. Their culture was an oral culture that relied heavily on memorization—far more than ours. Today, most of us have weak memories because we don't use them as much. We can look up anything on our phone, or Google, or Wikipedia, so we don't need to remember things. But ancient people depended on memory and could memorize not just small facts, quotes, and numbers but entire books. In fact, it wasn't uncommon for young Jewish boys to memorize the entire Torah, all eighty thousand words of the first five books of the Bible. It's likely that many Jews could accurately recall key details about Jesus' life and teachings, even well after his death. We may forget such things after a few years, but first-century Jews wouldn't.

Second, the gospels were written during the lifetime of Jesus' first followers. If someone just started making up stories about Jesus, or changing key facts, many contemporary people would have vigorously challenged them. They would have said, "No, that's not right! That's not what happened. I was there!" But we don't have any record of this happening. Instead, all the earliest accounts of Jesus seem to agree with each other, at least about the main events and teachings. For historians, this is extremely revealing. It's a strong sign those texts are accurate.

To use an analogy here, suppose someone wrote a book today denying that the Holocaust ever happened. Historians could challenge the book, pointing to pictures of the Holocaust, or evidence of the concentration camp buildings, or the shoes left by Nazi survivors, all to show that the

Holocaust really happened. However, the most powerful counterevidence would come from the people who *actually experienced* the Holocaust and are still alive today. Those people, who would have been children back then but can still remember it, would say, "No! You're wrong. I know the Holocaust really happened—I was there!" Well, the same thing is at play with the gospels. The Holocaust happened more than seventy-five years ago, but the gospels were written only forty to seventy years after the events they record. If living witnesses today could confirm the Holocaust, living witnesses in the late first century could certainly confirm Jesus' life, death, and teachings.

Finally, a third key is the letters of St. Paul, which speak often about Jesus' death and resurrection. Almost all of these letters were written before the first gospel, around the midfifties, only a couple of decades after Jesus' death. And they corroborate many events in the gospels, including his passion, death, and resurrection. So instead of forty to seventy years after the events, now we're talking approximately twenty years.

So you can use these three keys to explain why the time gap isn't troubling: first, that ancient Jews had extraordinary memories and could accurately recount events long after they happened; second, the gospels were recorded within the lifetime of witnesses who would ensure accuracy; and third, the letters of St. Paul, which corroborate the gospels, were written even earlier, within just a couple of decades after Jesus' death. These three facts affirm that the gap between the events and the gospels that record them isn't a significant problem.

Objection 3: "The gospels were passed down like the Telephone Game. Everything got twisted in transmission."

By now you know what to say: The Telephone Game is an extremely bad comparison. The purpose of the Telephone Game is to distort the message. The purpose of the gospels was to pass down real, accurate history. Also, unlike the Telephone Game, if people started distorting the gospel stories, living witnesses were around to correct them. And they would have. This analogy is simply a bad one.

Objection 4: "The gospels contain so many contradictions."

One skeptic has suggested there are more than one thousand contradictions in the Bible, such as how many women were at Jesus' tomb or how many angels appeared to them. You can respond to the objection saying that these purported contradictions are almost always apparent. They may seem contradictory at first glance, but only when taken out of context and without consideration for literary style. Even more, they almost never concern major doctrines or events—only minute details.

Yet even if it were true that the gospels contained contradictions, that would only make them similar to every other ancient historical document. Historians don't dismiss entire texts because they contain a handful of apparent

contradictions. Instead, they sift through the texts to determine which parts seem to be strongly historical and which
are dubious. Reading the four gospels together, we can
see that things like Jesus' basic teachings, his death on the
Cross, and his resurrection from the dead are uniformly
recorded, even if they differ in the minor details. So, you
can confidently say that key details about Jesus' life and
teaching are consistent in all four gospels.

Objection 5: "The gospels can't be historical, because they contain impossible events such as miracles."

Although skeptics won't usually admit this, most of them
reject the gospels because they contain miracles, especially
the grand miracle of all—Jesus' resurrection from the dead.
But skeptics can't simply dismiss the gospels on this basis
unless they have a prior view that miracles are, de facto,
impossible. Yet if that's what skeptics really believe, they
have to prove it. They have to offer some evidence or reasons to think that miracles are impossible. If skeptics offer
this objection, you can gently push back and say, "Well, why
do you discredit the gospels because they contain miracles?
Do you have any reasons for thinking miracles are impossible?" The point is to show that their rejection of the gospels
is based not on history or logic but on an intellectual prej-
udice against miracles.

Objection 6: "When studying Jesus, why do we only refer to Matthew, Mark, Luke, and John and not to any of the other gospel accounts?"

This objection is referring to the so-called gnostic or apocryphal gospels that have become popular in recent years, thanks in part to Dan Brown's *Da Vinci Code* and other publishers hoping to cash in on so-called hidden or lost gospels. Some of the most popular of these gospels include the Gospel of Thomas, the Gospel of Judas, and the Gospel of Peter.

Here's why most historians don't take these "hidden" gospels seriously: none of the other gospels are early; none stem from within the living memory of the eyewitnesses; and most were written centuries after Jesus' death. The earliest gnostic gospel we have, the Gospel of Thomas, is dated at the earliest to around AD 140, but the others were written far later than that, mostly in the late second, third, and fourth centuries. This means none of them could have been written by the people they're attributed to—people like Thomas, Judas, and Peter.

Also, these gnostic gospels are not "lives" of Jesus but mostly collections of sayings attributed to Jesus, so they don't tell us much about who Jesus was or what he did. And the sayings are often very strange. For example, at the end of the Gospel of Thomas, we see Jesus speaking about St. Mary Magdalene, and he says, "Look, I will guide her to make her male, so that she too may become a living spirit resembling you males. For every female who makes herself male will enter the domain of Heaven" (114:1–3). In other words, Jesus says women will only enter heaven if they become men. It's just not the sort of thing Jesus would say, and it doesn't align with everything else we know about Jesus. It's an obvious fabrication.

Finally, when you compare these gnostic gospels to the traditional four, you see obvious hints of legend and fabrication. For example, the Gospel of Peter has a brief episode describing Jesus' resurrection in which Jesus emerges from his tomb as a giant, with his head somehow higher than the clouds. And then from behind Jesus emerges a giant, walking, talking cross, which then has a conversation with God in heaven. Historians agree this is a legendary embellishment, and therefore we shouldn't take it as serious history.

When talking with skeptical friends or family, you can say that we trust the four traditional gospels more than any of the later gnostic gospels because they are early, historical accounts with no obvious signs of legend. The same can't be said of the gnostic texts.

So, now you should have clarity and confidence to respond to some of the best objections to the gospels.

RECOMMENDED BOOKS
(in order of importance)

Brant Pitre, *The Case for Jesus: The Biblical and Historical Evidence for Christ* (Image, 2016).

> Strongly recommended as the best book on what to say about the trustworthiness of the Bible. Pitre

highlights key content of his book in the Expert Interview, mentioned earlier in this chapter.

Craig Blomberg, *The Historical Reliability of the Gospels* (IVP Academic, 2007).

A scholarly and innovative study by an Evangelical; widely considered the gold standard in proving the reliability of the gospels.

Richard Bauckham, *Jesus and the Eyewitnesses: The Gospels as Eyewitness Testimony* (Eerdmans, 2017).

Demonstrates how the gospels are based on the firsthand oral testimony that gives access to the truth about the life of Jesus.

Trent Horn, *Hard Sayings: A Catholic Approach to Answering Bible Difficulties* (Catholic Answers Press, 2016).

Careful consideration and unraveling of apparent contradictions in scripture. Of special interest will be the chapter titled "Gospels That Can't Agree."

Michael Licona, *Why Are There Differences in the Gospels? What We Can Learn from Ancient Biography* (Oxford University Press, 2016).

Compares the gospels to Greco-Roman literature, especially Plutarch's *Lives*, to show why the gospels vary in their accounts of the same events.

FOR REFLECTION AND DISCUSSION

1. What might you say to someone who contends that the gospels are biased?
2. Why is it important to treat the gospels in the same way other ancient documents are treated?
3. Which objection to the gospels do you think is the strongest? Why? What might you say in response?
4. How would you respond to the assertion that the gospels were anonymously written and therefore unreliable?
5. Why is the Telephone Game a poor analogy for the handing down of the gospels?
6. How can we be sure the gospels are not myths?

FOR PRACTICE

For each of the following scenarios, write a response using what you learned in this chapter. Follow the directions in parentheses.

1. A skeptic says, "You're talking about Jesus and the apostles, but I don't think Jesus or the apostles existed. There's nothing outside the Bible to show they're real. You just believe myths." (Respond by demonstrating that the gospels record real historical persons and events.)
2. An atheist says, "Wait, so you're telling me you believe the gospels, which were translated dozens

of times and copied over and over again? That process just breeds corruption!" (Show from the chapter that translators and copiers of the gospels worked accurately.)

3. A college student says, "There have been social experiments done where something bizarre happens—for example, a clown bursts into a classroom and then runs away. Students cannot remember what happened, and their views contradict. How can witnesses remember what happened more accurately decades after the events?" (Explain why the early Christians could be reliable witnesses even years after the events.)

4

EXPLAINING THE EUCHARIST

In 1950, the young Catholic writer Flannery O'Connor was invited to a dinner party. She was a bit nervous since the party was hosted by Mary McCarthy, a widely esteemed writer, and it included many other movers and shakers. Throughout the party, O'Connor was worried she would embarrass herself in front of all these smart and cultured people.

Yet at some point during the evening, the discussion turned to the topic of the Eucharist. McCarthy, a fallen-away Catholic, said what she thought were a few kind words about it, noting how the Eucharist was a beautiful, powerful symbol, and "a pretty good one" at that.

The eyes in the room shifted slowly toward the young, nervous O'Connor, who everyone knew was Catholic. In a moment of great bluntness and clarity, she replied, "Well, if it's only a symbol, to hell with it!"

We can only imagine the awkward silence that followed that shocking reply!

But Flannery O'Connor was dead right. If the Eucharist is only a symbol or sign, if it's nothing more than that, then Catholics are guilty of something truly worthy of

hell—worshiping a piece of bread as if it were God. Because
in the Mass, the premiere act of worship for Catholics, that's
precisely what we do—join in worship before the Eucharist. Either Catholics are wrong about the Eucharist and are
deserving of hell, or they're right that the Eucharist really
is the Body and Blood of Jesus and the only appropriate
reaction is worship.

That's how serious the stakes are here, so that's why
we're tackling the question in this chapter. What is the
Eucharist? What did Jesus and the earliest Christians believe
about it? What does the Bible teach on the subject? And how
can we clearly explain the Eucharist to other people? How
can we confidently talk about it with friends and family,
especially non-Catholics, who think the Eucharist is, just as
Mary McCarthy thought, a beautiful symbol?

WHAT CATHOLICS BELIEVE ABOUT THE EUCHARIST

A Catholic social-science group named CARA, based at
Georgetown University, recently performed a huge survey of self-identified Catholics. One question they asked
was this: Which of the following statements best agrees
with your belief about the Eucharist? They had two options:
Option 1 was that Jesus Christ is really present in the bread
and wine of the Eucharist. Option 2 was that the bread and
wine are symbols of Jesus, but Jesus is not really present.

Only 57 percent of Catholics chose the first statement,
meaning 43 percent—nearly half—of these self-identified

Catholics thought the Eucharist was nothing more than a symbol of Jesus' presence.

Now, in the survey, the percentages changed dramatically depending on how often the person attended Mass. Around 90 percent of those who attended Mass weekly or more chose the first option, the real-presence view, while only 40 percent of those who attend Mass just a few times a year agreed with it. That makes sense. The more you believe the Eucharist is really Jesus, and not just a symbol, the more likely you are to attend Mass to receive the sacrament.

In any case, the survey highlights a monumental problem. If we're not clear about what the Eucharist is, then we're not clear on why the Mass is important or why we should even be Catholic. Many people are leaving the Church because they don't have any good reason to stay, as they don't believe in the Eucharist.

Let's begin, following our normal pattern, by examining what the Catholic Church actually teaches about the Eucharist. Hundreds of books have been written on this sacrament, examining it from all different perspectives. For instance, Bishop Robert Barron in his excellent book titled *Eucharist* looks at three angles: the Eucharist as sacred meal, the Eucharist as sacrifice, and the Eucharist as real presence. But it's only that last one we're focusing on here—the real presence of the Lord in the Eucharist—because that's the element that is most often in doubt, as the survey I mentioned above confirms.

The Catholic Church teaches three key truths about the Eucharist. First, Jesus told us literally to eat his flesh and drink his blood. Second, the bread and wine of Communion truly become the Body and Blood of Christ. Third, the bread and wine still look and taste like bread and wine, even after the consecration. Let's look at these facts one by one.

First, Jesus told us literally to eat his flesh and drink his blood. We'll dig deeper on this later, but for now I'll point you to the one place in the Bible where this is exceptionally clear—John 6. In this chapter, Jesus could not have been clearer about what he expects of his followers. He says, "Whoever eats my flesh and drinks my blood has eternal life, and I will raise him on the last day. For my flesh is true food, and my blood is true drink." Catholics take Jesus at his word here.

The second key belief is that the bread and wine of communion truly become the Body and Blood of Christ. Jesus told us to eat his flesh and drink his blood, but where do we find him? The earliest Christians recognized the answer in the celebration of Mass, which re-presents not only Christ's passion and death on the Cross but also the Last Supper. And it was at the Last Supper that Jesus broke the bread, saying to his disciples, "Take and eat; this is my body." And then he said of the wine, "Drink from it, all of you, for this is my blood of the covenant, which will be shed on behalf of many for the forgiveness of sins."

Again, the Catholic Church takes Jesus at his word here. Jesus didn't say, "Take and eat; this represents a sign of my body." He says, "Take and eat; this *is* my body." Catholics believe that when at Mass a priest, acting in the person of Christ, says those very same words of consecration, the bread and wine really become the Body and Blood of Jesus. They aren't just signs that represent Jesus; they truly become his body and blood.

This leads to the third key belief: the bread and wine still look and taste like bread and wine, even after the consecration. This, I think, is the big stumbling block for most people. The Catholic Church claims that the bread and wine at Mass truly become Jesus' body and blood, but the elements still look and taste like bread and wine.

To grasp what Catholics believe, we have to understand a technical process that philosophers call transubstantiation. Let's break that word down. Transubstantiation—"trans" means change, to change from one thing to another, and "substantiation" refers to substance, meaning the essence of something, what a thing *is*. So, transubstantiation means changing from one substance or essence to another.

Philosophers for thousands of years, dating at least back to Aristotle in the fourth century BC, distinguished between the substance of a thing and its accidents. A substance is what a thing fundamentally is, its essence, while its accidents are nonessential components. Let me give you a clear example. Consider a car. What is a car? What's the essence of a car? Most people would say a car is a motor vehicle with wheels used for transportation. That's the substance of a car, its essence. But of course cars can take many shapes, colors, and sizes and yet still be cars. All those attributes are accidental characteristics of the car. That's the difference between substance, what a thing fundamentally is, and accidents, its nonessential traits.

Now let's go back to the Eucharist. When the bread and wine turn into the Body and Blood of Christ at Mass, what's changing is the substance—what a thing is—and not the accidents—the nonessential traits. This means the bread and wine retain the appearance of mere food and drink, since the accidents stay the same, but the substance changes from bread to the Body of Christ, and from wine to the Blood of Christ.

But I'm guessing you already can anticipate a few objections, ones you've maybe already heard from Protestant friends and family members.

WHERE IS THAT IN THE BIBLE?

"Yeah, but where is that in the Bible?" This is probably the most common reply. Catholics, of course, love the Bible, and all of our beliefs, including the Eucharist, can be found either explicitly or implicitly in sacred scripture. But what do you say if a Protestant asks, "Where does scripture affirm this real presence?"

The Bible alludes to the Eucharist in many places, but we're going to concentrate on one single chapter, John 6, which is the single most important passage. Anytime you're trying to explain the Eucharist to someone, that should be your first, go-to source.

The second half of this chapter, which stretches from verses 22 through 71, is known as the "Bread of Life" discourse. Here Jesus is speaking to a large crowd in the synagogue in Capernaum. At first, the crowd tries to test him, implying that Moses gave a sign for the Israelites to believe in his authority, when through Moses, the Israelites received manna in the desert. Manna was mysterious, bread-like food supplied to the Israelites for forty years, as they wandered through the wilderness after fleeing Egypt. So Jesus' listeners essentially say, "If Moses gave our ancestors miraculous bread from heaven, what signs can *you* do to prove yourself?"

Jesus calmly replies, "Amen, amen, I say to you, it was not Moses who gave the bread from heaven; my Father gives you the true bread from heaven. For the bread of God is that which comes down from heaven and gives life to the world." The listeners are intrigued, and say, "Sir, give us this bread always."

Jesus responds: "I am the bread of life; whoever comes to me will never hunger, and whoever believes in me will never thirst." He adds, "I came down from heaven not to do my own will but the will of the one who sent me."

In response, the Jews begin murmuring. Murmuring is never a good sign. In biblical language, "murmuring" means not just whispering to the person next to you but expressing doubt and shock, sometimes even revulsion. You can detect their skepticism. They murmur among themselves, saying, "Is this not Jesus, the son of Joseph? Do we not know his father and mother? Then how can he say, 'I have come down from heaven?'"

And then here's where things get interesting. Jesus says, "Stop murmuring among yourselves." Then he says, "Amen, amen, I say to you, whoever believes has eternal life. I am the bread of life. Your ancestors ate the manna in the desert, but they died; this [and here you can imagine him pointing to himself] is the bread that comes down from heaven so that one may eat it and not die. I am the living bread that came down from heaven; whoever eats this bread will live forever; and the bread that I will give is my flesh for the life of the world."

You know there was a big silence after that. Did he really just say that? Did he just say he is the bread of life, who came down from heaven, and that if we eat his flesh, we will live forever? What in the world is he talking about?

The Jews scoff again, saying, "How can this man give us his flesh to eat?" which is actually a very good question. Besides the obvious strangeness of demanding that they eat his flesh, this command was especially repugnant to Jews, for their scripture prohibited the eating of human flesh.

At this point in the dialogue, we've reach a pivotal moment. Jesus' listeners are obviously shocked and scandalized, and Jesus has an opportunity to backtrack or tone down his language. He could have said, "No, no. You're misunderstanding me. I'm not saying you *actually* have to eat my flesh. I'm just speaking symbolically. Please don't take it literally!"

But he doesn't say that. Instead, he ratchets up his language. He intensifies it. He says, "Amen, amen, I say to you, unless you eat the flesh of the Son of Man and drink his blood, you do not have life within you. Whoever eats my flesh and drinks my blood has eternal life, and I will raise him on the last day. For my flesh is true food, and my blood is true drink. Whoever eats my flesh and drinks my blood remains in me and I in him . . . the one who feeds on me will have life because of me." You can imagine how troubling this language would have been!

In the Greek, Jesus uses two different words for "eat" in this passage. He begins with *phago* (pronounced *faygo*), a generic word for eating, but then later, when he cranks up his language, he switches to *trogo*, which means "to gnaw or chew." Similarly, instead of using the general word for body, *soma*, as if to say, "Eat my whole body from top to bottom," he uses the Greek word *sarx*, which refers specifically to the soft, fleshy skin that covers the body. In other words, he's saying in the most graphic language possible that we must gnaw and chew on his flesh, on his skin—he couldn't be more explicit.

All of this is just too much for his listeners. In fact, at this point, even his closest disciples begin to balk. Some of his own followers say, "This saying is hard; who can accept it?" But again, if they thought Jesus was speaking only at the symbolic level, why would this saying be hard to accept? Clearly, they recognized Jesus is literally asking them to eat his flesh and drink his blood.

And it's in their response that we come to one of the saddest lines in scripture: "As a result of this [hard teaching], many [of] his disciples returned to their former way of life and no longer accompanied him."

If there was ever a time when Jesus would want to clarify his words, when he would want to say, "Wait! No, don't leave! You're misunderstanding me! I'm not speaking literally!" then now was the time. The scriptures say that not just some but *many* of his disciples left over this teaching.

Yet once more, instead of softening his language, Jesus remains firm. He asks, "Does this shock you?" And then he asks his twelve apostles, "Do you also want to leave?" Then Peter, the great rock of the Church, offers his wonderful reply: "Master, to whom shall we go? You have the words of eternal life."

As you can see, John 6 offers the clearest, most unequivocal account of Jesus' desire for his followers to eat his flesh and drink his blood. It's clear from the text he was not speaking in symbolic or figurative language. He was speaking literally.

That Jesus wants us to consume his body and blood is clear from scripture. But there is still another question we must address: Even granting we're supposed to eat Jesus' flesh and drink his blood, what about the actual sacrament of the Eucharist, this thoroughly developed ritual? Is that mentioned anywhere in the Bible? Let's look at two significant sources.

First, all four gospel accounts describe Jesus celebrating the Last Supper, signaling that it's a central part of the Christian Gospel. In three of the accounts, we see Jesus holding up bread and saying, "Take it; this is my body," and of the wine, "This is my blood of the covenant, which will be shed for many," while encouraging his followers to continue repeating this ritual in his memory. John, writing near the end of the first century, assumes that Christians are already familiar with details of the Last Supper from the other gospels. So instead of repeating them, he reports Jesus' washing the disciples' feet and speaking about love and the Holy Spirit. And of course we've already studied John's teaching on the Eucharist in John 6.

Second, St. Paul describes the Eucharist in a few places, most notably in 1 Corinthians 11, where he presents the earliest text describing Jesus establishing the Eucharist:

> For I received from the Lord what I also handed on to you, that the Lord Jesus, on the night he was handed over, took bread, and, after he had given thanks, broke it and said, "This is my body that is for you. Do this in remembrance of me." In the same way also the cup, after supper, saying, "This cup is the new covenant in my blood. Do this, as often as you drink it, in remembrance of me" For as often as you eat this bread and drink the cup, you proclaim the death of the Lord until he comes. Therefore whoever eats the bread or drinks the cup of the Lord unworthily will have to answer for the body and blood of the Lord. (1 Cor 11:23–27)

Paul also says, "Whoever eats the bread or drinks the cup of the Lord unworthily will have to answer for the body and blood of the Lord." This strong language affirms the real presence of Christ in the Eucharist, and it's something Paul states matter-of-factly, as if he assumes his readers already believed.

So with all that in mind, here's the main thing to say when someone asks where to find the Catholic teaching of the Eucharist in the Bible. Point them to John 6, and walk them through it just as we've done in this chapter. You don't really need to do anything special. Just read through the passage with them and ask what Jesus could possibly mean other than literally to eat his body and drink his blood. If they balk, then walk them through the other passages above, especially 1 Corinthians 11:23–27.

EUCHARIST IN THE EARLY CHURCH

Peter Kreeft was a student at Calvin College, a major Protestant school, and was taking a history course there. During one class, his professor said he was going to explain the difference between Catholics and Protestants.

Protestants, he said, believed that Christ established a church as a boat to carry people to salvation. However, over time, especially in the Middle Ages, the boat had attracted barnacles, all sorts of manmade or even pagan accretions that were added on to the boat and slowed it down—rules, rituals, traditions, and so on. Thus, the Protestant Reformation was a period of cleansing, where the barnacles that the Catholic Church had added could be scraped off the original boat Christ had commissioned.

Catholics, the professor said, had a different perspective. They believed Christ established the Catholic Church from the start and that the doctrines and practices that Protestants saw as barnacles were, in fact, the very living and inseparable parts of the planks and beams of the ship. If you tried to scrape them away, you'd actually just tear the ship apart.

Those two explanations gave the young Kreeft a light-bulb moment. He realized that if these were the two options, it should be relatively easy to see which was right, because both hypotheses were empirically testable. He could simply look back to the history of the early Church, to Christians living in the first few hundred years after Christ, and see what they taught and believed. If the Protestant view was right, then the early Church would look like modern Protestantism—the original ship, cleansed of any barnacles. But if the Catholic view was right, the early Church would look similar to today's Catholic Church.

To his surprise, Kreeft discovered that the early Church was thoroughly Catholic and that if a Catholic and a Protestant from today took a time machine back to, say, AD 150, the Catholic would feel far more at home than the Protestant. The earliest Christians believed in the centrality of the Eucharist, the real presence, prayers to saints, devotion to Mary, and the offices of priest, bishop, and pope, among many other distinctively Catholic beliefs.

Most impressive is the nearly unanimous belief in the real presence of the Eucharist among Christian leaders through the centuries. I use the word *unanimous* not to exaggerate but as a statement of fact. With one exception—an eleventh-century monk named Berengar of Tours—every single Christian leader for the first fifteen hundred years of the Church accepted the real presence of Christ in the Eucharist.

Widespread disbelief in the real presence first occurred when Ulrich Zwingli, one of the early Protestant Reformers, denied it at the beginning of the sixteenth century. If Protestants are right that belief in the real presence is misguided, then for sixteen centuries all Christians were guilty of worshiping a piece of bread, thinking it was God. Consider how breathtaking that accusation is! It means that for sixteen centuries, every Christian was an idolater.

For a glimpse into what these early Christians believed, let's consider three great Christian writers who will give us confidence in the fact that the early Church believed in the real presence.

Ignatius of Antioch

First, around the year AD 110, we hear from Ignatius of Antioch. He was a disciple and friend of St. John the Apostle. Ignatius once criticized a group of heretics, saying, "They abstain from the Eucharist and from prayer, because they do not confess that the Eucharist is the flesh of our Savior Jesus Christ, flesh which suffered for our sins and which our Father, in His goodness, raised up again."[1] Ignatius could hardly be clearer. He's claiming that his opponents are heretics, in part because they don't believe the Eucharist is the flesh of Jesus Christ. And this is in AD 110 when people, like him, who were disciples of the apostles were still alive.

In another letter, Ignatius wrote, "I desire the Bread of God, which is the Flesh of Jesus Christ . . . and for drink I desire His Blood, which is love incorruptible."[2]

Justin Martyr

A second example is Justin Martyr, who wrote a letter around the year AD 150 that explains to the Roman emperor himself what Christians believe about the Eucharist. Justin says,

> We call this food Eucharist; and no one else is permitted to partake of it, except one who believes our teaching to be true. . . . For not as common bread nor common drink do we receive these; but since Jesus Christ our Savior was made incarnate by the word of God and had both flesh and blood for our salvation, so too, as we have been taught, the food which has been made into the Eucharist by the Eucharistic prayer set down by Him, and by the change of which our blood and flesh is nourished, is both the flesh and blood of that incarnate Jesus.[3]

Could Justin be clearer? The "food which has been made into the Eucharist . . . is both the flesh and blood of that incarnate Jesus."

Irenaeus of Lyons

A final quote comes from Irenaeus, who was a student of Polycarp, himself a disciple of John the Apostle. Irenaeus is writing in about the year AD 180 and says, "Jesus has declared the cup, a part of creation, to be His own Blood, from which He causes our blood to flow; and the bread, part of creation, He has established as His own Body, from which he gives increase to our bodies."[4]

This unanimity among the Church Fathers explains why even Martin Luther, the most influential of the Protestant Reformers, believed in the real presence of the Eucharist. In fact, Luther says, with typical rhetorical flourish, that only the devil, or those inspired by the devil, could possibly interpret "this is my body" to mean "this is just a sign of my body."[5]

Expert Interview with Joe Heschmeyer

► **Watch the interview here: https://claritasu.com/heschmeyer**

Joe Heschmeyer is a layman who serves at School of Faith, which sponsors pilgrimages and provides adult faith formation and one-on-one discipleship. Joe is best known for his blog *Shameless Popery* as well as his podcast, cleverly titled *The Catholic Podcast*.

In this interview, Joe responds to the following questions:

1. What are the basics every Catholic should know about the Eucharist?

2. What are some of the biggest misunderstandings that Catholics or others may have about the Eucharist?
3. How would you explain the meaning of the Eucharist to an atheist, an agnostic, or someone who's just indifferent?
4. What are the top objections a Protestant might give to the Eucharist, and how would you answer them?
5. Besides John 6, where else in the Bible can we find support for the Eucharist?
6. What is the significance of the fact that for the first thousand years, Christian leaders unanimously believed in the real presence?
7. What are some practical tips you recommend for talking about the Eucharist? What to say? What to avoid?

Excerpt from the Interview

"For both a Protestant and an atheist, I'd say, 'Well, God is obviously the one who caused the miracles of the Incarnation and the Eucharist. You can't say God is bound by the rules of science that he created.' This is a bizarre argument against miracles you'll sometimes hear, that they couldn't have happened since they're against nature. It's like, that's the whole point! The one who made nature can supersede it whenever he wants." (Joe Heschmeyer)

ANSWERING THE BEST OBJECTIONS

Let's turn our attention now to some of the best challenges and criticisms against the Catholic view of the Eucharist.

That way, when you hear these objections in person, you won't be surprised or alarmed. They'll be familiar to you and you'll know exactly how to answer them.

Objection 1: "Jesus spoke in metaphors all the time. He said, 'I am the door' and 'I am the vine,' so we shouldn't take him literally when he speaks about eating his body and drinking his blood."

This is the most common objection you'll hear. It claims that Catholics and others who believe in the real presence take Jesus too literally when it comes to the Eucharist, that he's probably just speaking symbolically.

So what should you say in response? There's no question that Jesus sometimes spoke in metaphors. But what matters here is whether Jesus was speaking metaphorically *when he taught about the real presence*. In reply you can say, "Yes, Jesus sometimes taught in metaphors, but not always, so we need to look at each statement on a case-by-case basis. And in the case of the Eucharist, the evidence is clear from both scripture and Church history that Jesus was *not* speaking metaphorically, and that's not how his disciples understood him."

Objection 2: "OK, well, in the particular case of John 6, Jesus is speaking symbolically about eating his flesh and drinking his blood."

What if someone drops the first objection, agreeing we need to look at Jesus' sayings on a case-by-case basis, but then they claim that *in this case*, with the Eucharist, Jesus was speaking symbolically? What should you say?

We should first compare John 6 with other places in the gospels where Jesus speaks about food. For instance, consider John 4:31–34, where Jesus' disciples tell him he needs to eat and Jesus responds, "I have food to eat of which you do not know." His disciples take his response literally. They think he has food hidden in his tunic. But Jesus corrects them, saying, "My food is to do the will of the one who sent me and to finish his work." So in this case, Jesus' disciples hear him speak about food and take him literally. But Jesus quickly corrects them, affirming that he was speaking not about literal food but about spiritual food—doing the will of his Father.

Next look at Matthew 16:5–12. There Jesus tells his disciples to "look out, and beware of the leaven." Confused, his disciples think Jesus is reprimanding them for forgetting to bring bread on their journey. But Jesus immediately corrects them, saying, "You of little faith, why do you conclude among yourselves that it is because you have no bread? Do you not understand? . . . How do you not comprehend that I was not speaking to you about bread? Beware of the leaven of the Pharisees and Sadducees." Again, we see Jesus speaking about food, and again his disciples take him literally. But then Jesus corrects them and says he was actually speaking metaphorically.

Now circle back around to John 6. Jesus speaks about food, saying they must eat his flesh and drink his blood to have eternal life. Take special note of verse 55 where Jesus says, "My flesh is true food and my blood is true drink." Once again, his disciples take him literally. They're disgusted and recoil at this hard teaching.

Yet here's the important twist: instead of correcting them, as Jesus does in the other two cases, he affirms his statements and ratchets up the language. Even when many of his disciples leave, he doesn't say, "Whoa, you're misunderstanding me!" This is strong confirmation that even though Jesus speaks symbolically elsewhere about food, in John 6 he literally means that Christians must eat his flesh and drink his blood.

Objection 3: "In John 6 the most important verse is 63, in which Jesus says, 'It is the spirit that gives life, while the flesh is of no avail. The words I have spoken to you are spirit and life.' This affirms that Jesus was not literally commanding us to eat his flesh, since 'the flesh is of no avail.' Instead, Jesus only wants us to believe in him, since his words are 'spirit and life.'"

This objection has a couple of problems. First, interpreting verse 63 this way would contradict the entire series of verses before it. Why would Jesus repeatedly command his disciples to "eat my flesh" and "drink my blood" but then, as a conclusion, say that doing so would be of no avail? That just wouldn't make sense, so we know that can't be the right interpretation.

Second, when Jesus says that "the flesh is of no avail," he doesn't mean flesh in our contemporary sense. He's not saying the body is worthless. He's using the word in a different way. For first-century Jews, "flesh" referred to the corrupted, base way of seeing and behaving (this is why Paul can both love the human body and routinely criticize "the flesh").

Third, Jesus is not saying *his* flesh is of no value, contradicting everything he just said about eating his body. He's saying *the* flesh is of no avail, that our corrupted faculties can't by themselves lead us to eternal life. Instead, Jesus says, we need to transcend our fleshy desires and follow his words about eating his body and drinking his blood, for he provides spirit and life.

Objection 4: "If Catholics eat Jesus' body and blood, then they are guilty of cannibalism, which the Bible clearly condemns."

This false interpretation is precisely why so many followers left Jesus. They were convinced that when Jesus spoke about eating his flesh and drinking his blood, he wanted them to gnaw on his physical skin and drink his body fluid. But Jesus isn't commanding cannibalism. The Eucharist is different from cannibalism in at least three important ways.

First, cannibals eat ordinary human flesh. But in the Eucharist, Catholics don't eat the ordinary human flesh and blood of Jesus. They consume the glorified, resurrected body of Christ. Eating a mere man would be cannibalism, but consuming the glorified, risen body of God is not the same.

Second, cannibals eat the reality of human flesh under the appearance of flesh. Remember what we learned about substance and accident, or reality and appearance. Catholics consume the body of Christ under the *appearances* of bread and wine. This is a major difference from cannibalism.

Third, if Catholics were really guilty of cannibalism, then Protestants would be too. Most Protestants celebrate communion but believe they are only symbolically consuming the body and blood of Christ. Yet if the Eucharist is cannibalism, that would mean they're taking part in symbolic cannibalism. But we know Christ would never command his disciples to take part, even symbolically, in an evil like cannibalism, even symbolically. That can't possibly be the right interpretation.

So now you know what to say in response to the four most common objections you'll hear regarding the real presence of the Eucharist. In the next section, you'll learn some helpful tips on how to discuss the topic.

TALKING POINTS AND TIPS

Tip 1: Keep the focus on John 6.

John 6 is the clearest biblical description of the Eucharist. Jesus says multiple times that in order to have eternal life, we must eat his flesh and drink his blood. When talking to people, you want to keep coming back to this passage. In fact, you might consider opening up John 6 in a print Bible, or pulling it up on your phone or computer, and reading through it together with your dialogue partner. Then ask,

"What do you think about it?" You might say, "It seems pretty clear to me that Jesus is saying we must eat his flesh and drink his blood, which is what we Catholics believe happens in the Eucharist at Mass. But what do you think Jesus is referring to here?" Give them a chance to offer an alternative explanation; otherwise, help them to affirm that Jesus really means what he says.

Tip 2: Show how John 6 is different than times when Jesus speaks symbolically.

If the person does offer an alternative explanation, chances are high they'll claim Jesus is just speaking symbolically. But we have decided that can't be the case for two reasons. First, you can explain that in other places where Jesus speaks symbolically about food, and his disciples take him literally, he is quick to correct them. But in John 6 his disciples take him literally and he does not correct them. He affirms the literal interpretation.

Second, you can say that if Jesus is speaking symbolically in John 6, we would expect many of the earliest Christians to understand him that way. But none of them did for the first thousand years, which is a big strike against the symbolic interpretation.

Tip 3: Ask them to point to one Christian in the first thousand years of the Church who denied the real-presence view.

This is a loaded challenge, because no answer is available. There simply isn't any Christian from the first thousand years who denied the real presence. But if Jesus was speaking symbolically, this means every single Christian for at least ten centuries misunderstood this critical doctrine and was probably guilty of idolatry for worshiping a piece of bread. Few Christians are willing to make such an egregious accusation.

Some critics may point to an eleventh-century French monk, Berengar of Tours, as one example of a Christian who denied the real presence before the Reformation. However, first, his denial is debatable, as it's unclear precisely what Berengar of Tours believed about the Eucharist; second, he's the only outlier; and third, even if Berengar of Tours did deny the real presence, he did so in the eleventh century. That's why you want to be sure to challenge the person you're talking with to point to any figure in the *first thousand years* of Christianity who denied the real presence. That's the challenge that can't possibly be met.

Tip 4: Help them desire to believe in the real presence.

This was very important to me during my own conversion from Protestantism to Catholicism. I can't remember what prompted it, but something challenged me to wonder whether I *wanted* the real presence to be true. In other words, did I *desire* that Christ could be really present in bread and wine? As a Protestant Christian who loved Jesus, I started to realize that I at least wanted this doctrine to be true, and that set me on a new path of openness.

Sometimes, when introducing a new and counterintuitive view to people, it's best to start by helping them *want* that view to be true before trying to defend it logically. This usually changes them and makes them more open-minded.

On the other hand, if they say, "No, I don't have any desire for that. I don't want it to be true," that's a sign there is something else holding them back—some emotional or personal hang-up you may have to deal with first.

For how could any Christian who loves the Lord Jesus, and wants to unite with him as deeply as possible, not at least *want* the real-presence view to be true? How could they not agree that the certainty of the real presence is, all things considered, more desirable than the merely symbolic view? So ask them whether they *want* the real presence to be true, and help them see how wonderful it is. This will lower their defenses and help them explore the question with a more open mind.

Tip 5: Recommend a good book on the real presence.

There are many Catholic teachings that are easy to communicate through a single conversation or two, but I've found when talking with Protestant friends and family that the Eucharist takes a little more study. It's just such a profound teaching and paradigm shift for most non-Catholics.

Usually, the person needs to spend considerable time thinking about it, or going through a good book that carefully shows how Catholics read John 6 or what the Church Fathers thought about the Eucharist. You might choose one of the book recommendations below and pass it on to them.

RECOMMENDED BOOKS
(in order of importance)

Trent Horn, *20 Answers: Eucharist* (Catholic Answers Press, 2017).

> This booklet addresses questions and objections on the Eucharist and not only considers the biblical evidence for the doctrine but also expands the focus to practical questions, such as "Can non-Catholics receive the Eucharist?"

Bishop Robert Barron, *Eucharist* (Orbis Books, 2008).

> Beautiful and helpful, this is the best full-length book on the topic. Bishop Barron approaches the Eucharist from three perspectives: as sacred meal, as sacrifice, and as real presence.

Scott Hahn, *The Lamb's Supper: The Mass as Heaven on Earth* (Doubleday, 1999).

> A modern classic that shows through the book of Revelation how the celebration of the Mass participates mystically in the eternal supper of the Lamb. Especially helpful for Protestants.

Brant Pitre, *Jesus and the Jewish Roots of the Eucharist: Unlocking the Secrets of the Last Supper* (Image, 2011).

> An inspiring and insightful look at the Last Supper, demonstrating that the Eucharist is the culmination of many Jewish events and beliefs, from the Passover, to the manna in the desert, to the Bread of Presence in the Temple.

FOR REFLECTION AND DISCUSSION

1. When asked why Catholics believe in the Eucharist, what would you say?
2. Why is John 6 such a convincing text demonstrating the real presence?
3. In addition to John 6, where in the Bible can you find evidence for the Eucharist?
4. How would you explain and illustrate the meaning of transubstantiation to a Protestant?
5. If someone asked you for proof that early Christians believed the Eucharist is the Body and Blood of Jesus, how would you respond?
6. If someone accused you of cannibalism because you ate the body and drank the blood of Christ, how would you defend yourself?
7. How might you help someone desire to believe in the real presence?

FOR PRACTICE

For each of the following scenarios, write a response using what you learned in this chapter. Follow the directions in parentheses.

1. A member of your parish has stopped receiving Communion and is considering leaving the Church. She says she cannot believe that the wafer and the chalice of wine are really the Body and Blood of Christ. A

Fundamentalist Protestant has been telling her that when Jesus said to eat his body and drink his blood, he was speaking symbolically and that it was the devil who made Catholics believe he really meant it literally. (What arguments might you use to correct her view?)

2. A non-Catholic Christian friend objects, "The doctrine of transubstantiation did not come about until around the twelfth century. Medieval theologians discovered Aristotle and brought his analysis of substance in line with Catholic dogma. So, Catholics cannot possibly claim their doctrine of the Eucharist was taught in the early Church, unless we count the twelfth century as early!" (How could you respond to this?)

5

ABORTION

UNDERSTANDING THE ABORTION ISSUE

Key Terms

The goal of this chapter is to provide a clear understanding of abortion, and we should start by defining our terms. Let's start with *abortion*. Abortion is the direct, intentional killing of an unborn human. Each of those words is important. Abortion is direct because it doesn't involve the child dying as the result of an indirect procedure. And it's intentional because that's what both the mother and the doctor both intend. The death of the child is the direct, intended result.

What about *fetus*? Fetus is a medical term referring to a particular stage of development among humans. If you remember from biology class, a mother's egg is fertilized by the father's sperm, resulting in a new human organism, called a *zygote*. The zygote rapidly develops over the next couple of weeks into an *embryo*. Then about eight weeks later, after the major organs and body parts are in place, the embryo moves into the next stage and is called a *fetus*, a term used from that point until birth. So basically, the unborn child is a *zygote* for the first couple of weeks, an *embryo* during the next eight weeks, and then a *fetus* for the last roughly thirty weeks of pregnancy until birth.

When discussing abortion, some pro-abortion people prefer to talk about aborting a fetus, because it sounds less troubling than aborting a child or aborting a baby. But instead of *fetus*, you can use more humanizing terms such as aborting "a human being," "an unborn child," or simply "the unborn." Those are all interchangeable and all are accurate ways to speak about the little human being growing inside her mother.

Let's look at two more terms: *pro-life* and *pro-choice*. In general, *pro-life* identifies people who promote the life of unborn children. They aim to prevent unborn children from being killed. On the other hand, *pro-choice* identifies people who promote the option of a mother to decide whether to abort her unborn child. Not all pro-choicers are pro-abortion, and it's not fair to equate the two. Some aggressively promote abortion, but others just think women should be able to *choose* whether to have abortions.

The key thing to remember is that both *pro-life* and *pro-choice* are loaded terms and can mean different things to different people. So when you're talking with people who identify as one or the other, don't assume you know what they mean. Ask them, "OK, just so I'm clear, when you say you're *pro-choice*, what do you mean?" Then ask follow-up questions to further clarify their view. The key is to understand what the other person believes instead of settling for labels. That's a first step before trying to change anyone's mind.

Types of Abortion

Now that we understand the key terms involved in the abortion debate, let's discuss what happens in an abortion. What does it involve? I won't go into all the details here. You can find that online, and I encourage you to read about it. Researching abortion will galvanize you to fight for unborn children, given how gory the process is. Briefly, there are three main types of abortion.

Abortion pills. This procedure involves the mother taking a drug that kills the unborn child. This accounts for around 20 percent of all abortions. The pills cause the fetus to detach from the uterine wall, depriving it of blood and nourishment, thus killing it. This method of abortion is usually performed during the first seven to ten weeks of pregnancy.

Suction abortion. This accounts for about 75 percent of all abortions, making it by far the most common method. In this procedure, the doctor inserts a tube into the woman's uterus and sucks the unborn child out. And yes, it's as awful as it sounds. The vacuum force is ten to twenty times stronger than your household vacuum, and the force violently tears apart the unborn child's tiny, fragile body.

Dilation and Evacuation (D&E). About 5 to 10 percent of abortions are done through a procedure known as D&E. In this method the abortionists put a long clamp into the uterus and rip off the child's arms, legs, and other body parts piece by piece, until they have removed them all. Then he has to reassemble the baby on the table to be sure he has not left any parts in the mother's womb. I have to be honest with you—this is one of the most gruesome things I've ever read about. This unbelievably distressing procedure alone is enough to spur you to protect the unborn.

There are other, less common types of abortion, including dilation and extortion (D&X), commonly known as partial-birth abortion. This procedure involves partly delivering the child feet first and then crushing the child's skull while it's still in the birth canal.

Now, I know these descriptions are distressing. But it's important we know exactly what abortion involves. These descriptions aren't meant to scare you or play on your emotions. They're simply putting reality on display. I've found that many of my pro-choice friends don't actually understand what abortion involves—and this includes some people who have had abortions themselves! Once they learn how violent and gruesome these procedures are, and see pictures of what really happens, many of them rethink their support of abortion.

Statistics

How many abortions are performed each year? What's the scale we're talking about? Since the infamous *Roe v. Wade* decision in 1973, which effectively legalized abortion, roughly one million abortions have occurred annually in the United States. That's about 2,800 abortions every single day for the last forty-five years. In fact, and this statistic always makes me gulp, about a third of women by age forty-five will have had at least one abortion. So if you're walking down the street, chances are that one out of every three adult women you see will have had an abortion.

Reasons for Abortion

Why do women have abortions? By far, the two most common reasons women give for having an abortion are social and economic. According to the Guttmacher Institute, Planned Parenthood's former research arm, 74 percent of women say that "having a baby would dramatically change my life." And 73 percent say that "I can't afford a baby right now."

Abortion Laws

How about the current laws surrounding abortion? Before 1973, abortion was illegal virtually everywhere. But in 1973, the Supreme Court handed down its pivotal *Roe v. Wade* decision. *Roe v. Wade* divided pregnancy into three twelve-week trimesters, and it ruled that in the first two trimesters states were no longer allowed to outlaw abortion. It was now a legal right to have an abortion during the first two trimesters. (States could at least regulate the procedure in the second trimester to ensure the health of the mother.)

Roe v. Wade did allow states to ban abortion in the third trimester or the last twelve weeks of pregnancy, but it did not require it, and it said that if states outlawed third-trimester abortions, they had to allow an exception for abortions when deemed necessary by the doctor. But a companion case, *Doe v. Bolton*, contended that the word *necessary* wasn't clear enough and could be open to many interpretations.

The Supreme Court responded by ruling that "medical judgment may be exercised in the light of all factors—physical, emotional, psychological, familial, and the woman's age—relevant to the well-being of the patient. All these factors may relate to health."[1] In other words, almost any abortion could be deemed "necessary" under this definition. In effect, abortion was now legal in the third trimester, just as it was in the first two.

Many states have since made laws trying to lower the number of abortions by adding stipulations to the *Roe v. Wade* ruling. For example, some states now require minors to notify their parents before obtaining an abortion, or to get an ultrasound and see their unborn child, which typically reduces the number of abortions. But the sad fact is that in virtually every state, a woman who wants an abortion can get one legally.

There is some hope the Supreme Court will reverse the *Roe v. Wade* decision in the future. Many legal scholars, including pro-choice scholars, believe that strictly from a legal perspective *Roe v. Wade* was a badly reasoned decision. If *Roe v. Wade* was overturned, however, it would only send authority back to the states. That would not make abortion universally illegal. Each state would then have to decide whether to restrict abortion and in what way. Reversing *Roe v. Wade* would be an important step, but even that wouldn't resolve the issue. What we need is to have conversations on the ground, with our family and friends, to change people's hearts and minds.

THE ONE KEY QUESTION

When you're discussing abortion, only one question matters: Are the unborn human? That's the key question that divides people on abortion. If the unborn are not human, then abortion would be just like smacking a mosquito or taking medicine to kill off some bacteria. It would not be immoral, and it would be no problem. But if the unborn are human, then abortion would involve taking an innocent human life, and there could be no greater immoral act than that.

So the whole conversation hinges on that one question. Although friends and family may raise numerous other considerations, such as rape, incest, bodily rights, and so on, all those things are secondary to the main question: Are the unborn human? Lock that question in your mind so that when you are discussing abortion you have a sure center point to return to. Keep bringing the conversation back to that key question.

The Ten-Second Pro-Life Apologist Strategy

But how do you help people answer that question? How do you affirm that the unborn are human beings worth protecting? The best approach I know comes from the pro-life advocate Steve Wagner. He calls it the "ten-second pro-life apologist" strategy. It's made of up three questions that you can ask someone in less than ten seconds. Here they are:

First, if it's growing, isn't it alive?

Second, if it has human parents, isn't it human?

Third, human beings such as you and me are valuable, aren't we?

The first question relies on basic science. It's an indisputable fact that at the moment of conception, when a male sperm fertilizes a female egg, a new living organism is created that begins to grow and develop.

The second question is also a scientific fact. This new organism has human parents and human DNA, so it can't be anything other than human. Now it may be a very small, undeveloped human, but it's still a living, growing, *human* organism. (If someone denies that, you can calmly reply, "Well, if it's not human, what species is it?")

Finally, the third question is meant to suggest that all human beings have an equal right to life. Here you might get a little pushback. People might contend that all humans are valuable, but the unborn are *not* like you and me. They may claim the unborn are less human than born people, and thus less valuable. They might think humanity slides along a spectrum, so that you can be less human, more human, or fully human.

If that's the case, then your goal is to convince the other person that humanity is binary. Humanity is like pregnancy, in this sense. You're either pregnant or you're not. Although we sometimes say colloquially, "Wow, she's so pregnant!" the reality is you can't be a "little bit pregnant"—you're either pregnant or not. Similarly, you can't be a "little bit human." You're either human or not. And if this is true, then the unborn human is actually just as human as any other human being. They're just as human as an infant, a toddler, a teenager, a young adult, or a senior citizen. They're all equally human, even though they're at different stages of development.

Demonstrating the Humanness of the Unborn

But how do we demonstrate this? How do we convince someone that the unborn child is just as valuable as the toddler, teenager, young adult, or senior citizen? Well, you just have to remember a simple acronym: SLED. Maybe picture a small child riding a sled down a snowy hill, which is how I stick it in my mind.

SLED stands for size, level of development, environment, and dependency. These are the only four ways an unborn child differs from other humans. Your goal is to show why these differences are only arbitrary differences, such as age or hair color, and that they don't affect the humanity of the unborn; they don't make them any less human. Let's go through the terms of SLED one by one.

Size. Someone might say, "How can something so small be a person? After conception, the embryo is just a clump of cells!" In response, you want to affirm exactly what Dr. Seuss says in *Horton Hears a Who*: "A person's a person, no matter how small."

Size is irrelevant to whether someone is a human being. And you can prove this by asking the other person, "Is a toddler less of a human than a teenager, since the toddler is much smaller?" "Of course not," they'll say. "They're both equally human." Or you might ask, "How big must an unborn child become to be really considered human?"

That will be tough for them to answer because most people know that very small people and very large people are equally human.

Level of development. Level of development is also irrelevant to whether someone is human. A critic might say, "Well, the fetus can't think or feel pain. It doesn't have a fully developed brain." But this same reasoning can apply to many born people who have developmental disabilities and can't think properly or feel pain. Are these people less human than the rest of us? Or consider this: scientists tell us that our brains don't fully develop until around age twenty-five. Does that mean everyone under twenty-five is less human than older adults? Individuals may be less-developed human beings, but they're still human beings. And they still have a right to life.

Environment. Where someone resides is also irrelevant to whether the person is human. Someone might say, "The fetus isn't in the world yet. It doesn't even breathe air." But they are in the world; they're just hidden from view. They're developing inside the womb of their mother, which is the exact environment they're supposed to be in at their stage of development. It doesn't matter whether a human lives in a house, an igloo, an incubator, or a womb. It's still human regardless of its environment. You don't lose the right to live based on *where* you live.

Dependency. A critic might contend that the unborn are not fully human because they're completely dependent on another human being to live—namely, their mother. You can respond in a couple of ways. You might want to draw attention to born people who are dependent on others to live. For instance, you could mention people with disabilities or elderly people who are close to death and depend on others to live.

Or you may use an analogy to show why being dependent doesn't remove your right to life. Here's one I like to use: Suppose two scuba divers are exploring an underwater cave, when the first diver's oxygen tank breaks. He can survive only if he gets air from the second diver's tank, and let's assume the second diver has enough oxygen for both of them. The first diver is completely dependent on the second diver. Does that fact give the second diver the right to pull out a knife and kill the first diver, because of his dependency? Of course not! In fact, we'd say the second diver has a *duty* to share his oxygen, especially since he has plenty to spare, making the sacrifice minimal.

The same thing holds for unborn children. A person's humanity does not change based on their degree of dependency. You don't become less human the more you depend on others.

To recap so far, we learned that the key question in the abortion debate is "Are the unborn human?" We saw how to make the case that the unborn *are* human by using the ten-second pro-life argument: If it's growing, isn't it alive? If it has human parents, isn't it human? And human beings are valuable, aren't they? And then we discussed how to use the SLED strategy to show that differences—size, level of development, environment, and dependency—do not matter when it comes to determining human value.

But what about the situation where someone agrees that the unborn are human but still thinks there are cases in which abortion is justified? Let's talk about that next.

TROT OUT THE TODDLER

The best strategy to persuade people that abortion is *always* wrong, regardless of the circumstances, is called "trot out the toddler." The version I'll share comes from Trent Horn, but it originates with the pro-life apologist Scott Klussendorf.

Here's how it works. When someone gives you a reason they think abortion is justified, you want to show how that same reason can justify killing a two-year-old toddler. And since nobody thinks it's OK to kill an innocent two-year-old, we can show that the reason they gave must be flawed and should not justify abortion.

This is a type of argument known as a *reductio ad absurdum*. Quick philosophy lesson: In a *reductio ad absurdum*, you take the other person's principle and apply it to a situation that, when worked out logically, has absurd ramifications. The point is to show that if you want to hold that principle, you also have to embrace an absurd outcome. But if, like most people, you want to avoid the absurd outcome, then you have to give up the principle too.

This may seem a bit abstract, so let's illustrate the "trot out the toddler" strategy with an example.

You first want to ask a pro-choice person why they think abortion should be acceptable, and they might say something like, "Well, I think if the child is unwanted, or will be raised in poverty or harsh circumstances, then the mother should be allowed to prevent that child from coming into this miserable world and having an awful life." Your response is to apply that same principle to justify aborting a two-year-old (you "trot out the toddler"). You might say, "OK, I see where you're coming from. And I agree with you that it's awful for any child to be raised in poverty. We should do everything we can to help poor mothers and children. But let me ask you this: Suppose I have a two-year-old right here next to me, and his family is extremely poor. He's being raised by a single mother who has no money or energy to care for him. Suppose the child lives in a deeply dysfunctional neighborhood, on a street filled with gang violence and drugs and with bullets flying by every night. If his situation is that awful, should his mother just be allowed to kill him, to prevent his misery?"

The overwhelming majority of people will say, "No, of course not. The mother shouldn't kill her two-year-old kid." Smart opponents will usually see where you're going at this point, but go ahead and make the connection for them. Say, "I agree with you. The mother *shouldn't* kill her two-year-old simply because he lives in difficult circumstances. But if the unborn are just as human as toddlers, then why is it OK to kill them for that reason? Why is it *wrong* to kill two-year-olds who *definitely* live in bad circumstances, but it's OK to kill the unborn who only *might* live in bad circumstances?"

Now, at this point, one of two things will happen. Either the person will see the problem and admit you have a good point, that we shouldn't kill a child just because the child lives in a difficult situation. But sometimes they'll push back and say, "Well, that's not a good analogy. The unborn are different than two-year-olds because . . . ," and they'll try to break the analogy by suggesting some important difference. For example, they may say that "the unborn are different than two-year-olds because they can't feel pain," or the "unborn aren't conscious," or "the unborn don't have fully developed brains," or "the unborn aren't born yet." And in that case, now you turn back to the SLED strategy to show why all those differences are irrelevant when it comes to the question of human value.

I'll give you a few more examples so you can see this in action. Suppose the other person says, "The fetus isn't fully developed yet so it's not really human." Then you might say, "Well, a two-year-old isn't fully developed yet, so should its mother have the right to kill it?"

Or someone might say, "Women should have the right to choose," to which you could reply, "I agree that in many cases women should be free to decide how to act. But let me ask you this: Should a woman have a right to choose to kill her two-year-old toddler?"

Or they might say, "Well, the fetus is dependent on the mother to live, and nobody has a right to use the mother's body." Then you can say, "Well, the two-year-old is dependent on his or her mother to live too. So shouldn't the mother have the right to kill her child because he depends on her body and energy?"

As you can see, most of these objections turn back to our original one key question: "Are the unborn human?" It might be true that the unborn feel less pain, are not conscious, don't have fully developed brains, or haven't been born yet. But none of that really matters if they are human beings, as human as you, me, or any two-year-old. If the unborn are innocent human beings like us, then no reason can justify directly killing them.

Let's sum up the strategy. Step 1: Identify why the other person supports abortion. Step 2: Show why that reason would also justify killing a two-year-old. Step 3: Show that if we wouldn't kill a two-year-old for that reason, we shouldn't kill the unborn for that reason either. And step 4: If they push back and contend that the unborn are significantly different than two-year-olds, go back to the one key question: "Are the unborn human?" and show why the unborn are every bit as human as two-year-olds, using the SLED strategy we learned earlier.

Expert Interview with Trent Horn

➤ **Watch the interview here: https://claritasu.com/horn**

Trent Horn is an author, a speaker, and a staff apologist for Catholic Answers. He holds master's degrees in theology and philosophy and is pursuing a third in bioethics. On the weekly radio program *Catholic Answers Live*, Horn dialogues with atheists, pro-choicers, and other non-Catholic callers. He is the author of seven books, including *Persuasive Pro-Life: How to Talk about Our Culture's Toughest Issue* (Catholic Answers, 2014), and is the host of *The Counsel of Trent* podcast.

In this interview, Horn responds to the following questions:

1. How did you get involved with pro-life work, and why is abortion such a pressing issue for you?
2. What should we say to someone who says, "Let's just agree to disagree about abortion"?
3. How can we respond to pro-choice supporters who admit the unborn are human but say they're just *biologically* human, not yet human *persons* who have rights?
4. What can you say to a pro-choicer who says they do not know when an unborn human becomes a person?
5. What approach should we take when you're talking with someone who seems fine with infanticide?
6. What can you say to someone who argues that twinning shows that life does not begin at conception?
7. What advice would you give to a person who has had an abortion?
8. What is the biggest mistake pro-lifers make when discussing abortion, and how do we avoid it?

Excerpt from the Interview

"I like to ask people who say the unborn are not human, 'Look, are you comfortable making the same kind of argument other people have made in the past in favor of oppression?' Their argument goes something like this, 'Well, these Native

Americans are human, but they're not persons. . . . These Jews are human, but they're not persons. . . . Your argument is similar to theirs. Does that concern you at all?'" (Trent Horn)

HOW TO DISCUSS THE HARD CASES

Chances are high that when you talk with a pro-abortion advocate, they will ask, "Well, what about a woman who is raped and gets pregnant? Or what about cases of incest? Or what about when the baby will have serious health defects? Or what about when the pregnant woman's life is in jeopardy?"

Most people struggle with these hard cases, even if they think abortion is wrong. In fact, when you look at surveys about abortion, the most popular view in America is that abortion should be generally illegal except in the cases of rape, incest, or when the baby's or mother's health is in danger. Since that's the most common view, you have to be ready to discuss these hard cases.

Before getting into each case, keep in mind that these "hard case" objections can often be smokescreens. Sometimes pro-choice people will throw out the hardest cases— rape, incest, and health dangers—in order to undermine the pro-life case, but really what they want is *unlimited* access to abortion at all stages and for all reasons, not just in the hard cases.

So when someone brings up the hard cases, the first thing you should say is, "OK, let's just suppose, for the sake of argument, that I agree with you and I admit abortion should be legal in the cases of rape, incest, and health dangers. But those cases are extremely rare, accounting for only 2 to 4 percent of all abortions. At least 96 percent of abortions are elective, meaning the mother chooses to abort for financial, emotional, or other personal reasons, not because of rape, incest, or health. So, if I agreed to permit abortions for the 2 to 4 percent of hard cases, would you join me and agree we should ban abortions in the 96 percent of other cases?"

Their answer to that question will be telling. If they say yes, then you've found common ground, and you can ask them the natural follow-up question: "Great! But why do you think we should ban abortion in the other 96 percent of cases? What's wrong with those?" This will ultimately drive the conversation back to the one key question: "Because the unborn are human, and therefore abortion kills an innocent human being."

But if they say they won't join you in opposing the other 96 percent of abortion cases, then you know the hard cases are really just a smokescreen. It's not that the person is worried solely about those hard cases. It's that the person wants abortion to be legal in all cases, for all reasons. And if that's true, you don't need to focus only on the hard cases. You can say, "Well, it seems then that your problem isn't just with these hard cases. You think abortion should be legal for *all* reasons, right?" Then just use the other tips and this chapter to discuss abortion in general—ask them the one key question, then trot out the toddler, and then use the SLED strategy.

But let's assume the person is uncomfortable about abortion, but he or she isn't sure what to make of these hard cases. The person thinks abortion is wrong in general and that in a perfect world there wouldn't be any abortions. Nevertheless, this person still believes that in these hard cases, abortion is justified. For that scenario, let's walk through the hard cases one by one, so you'll know exactly how to handle them.

Rape

The first thing you want to do is affirm that rape is awful. You can't say that enough. It's one of the most egregious crimes in the world, so do not downplay that fact. A woman who suffers rape is always the victim, and it is never her fault. But once that has been made clear, you want to add that it's also not the fault of the child who might have resulted from that act. The only person who should be punished is the rapist, and he should be punished with the harshest available penalties. The woman certainly shouldn't be punished, and neither should the unborn child if the woman becomes pregnant. Why should an innocent child have to die because of a crime committed by someone else?

Some people might say, "Yeah, but how could you force that poor woman to carry the baby to term? Every time she sees that child she'll be reminded of the man who raped her!" I agree it's an almost unimaginable difficulty for a woman to give birth to and raise a child who was fathered by a man who raped her. It enrages me just thinking about it. But again, the solution to such a problem is not to murder the child. The child did nothing wrong. He's as innocent as his mother. The solution to one evil act of rape is not to commit another evil act of murder.

You can also use the "trot out the toddler" strategy here and say, "Well, suppose the mother did give birth to the rapist's child, but around the child's second birthday, the mother realizes that after two years, she just can't take it anymore. The child is looking more and more like her rapist, and it's causing her immense trauma and pain. Should she then have the right to kill the two-year-old?" Most people would say no. If nothing else, she should give the child up for adoption or ask relatives to help care for the child. But then the same principles should also apply to an unborn child, which is every bit as human and deserving of life as the two-year-old. So, to handle this objection about rape, emphasize the evil of the crime but also maintain that the unborn child is innocent and does not deserve to die for the crimes of someone else.

Incest and Health of the Baby

Let's take these two hard cases together because they're usually based on the same objection: "What if the child is going to be born with severe birth defects or disabilities? Shouldn't we prevent it from having a life of misery?"

First, ask abortion advocates to consider what this says to people born with disabilities. For example, tell them to think about the men and women in the Special Olympics. I challenge anyone to go to a Special Olympics event and tell those people, "Well, it probably would have been better if you had been aborted." It's crazy beyond imagining! We have innumerable examples of people living amazing lives and flourishing despite birth defects or disabilities.

Second, try to convince your pro-abortion friend that a person's value is not tied to his health or productivity. This false perspective is a serious problem in our culture today. In truth, people are valuable simply because God made them with infinite human dignity. That dignity doesn't change whether a child has Down syndrome or will be born with only nine fingers or one leg. Nor does their value change even if they die right after being born. We should protect and cherish the disabled, not kill them prematurely. Nothing justifies killing an innocent child.

Health of the Mother

Here are a few things to keep in mind about this complicated concern.

Abortion Is Never the Medical Solution

First, there is no medical problem for which abortion is the only solution. If someone tries to tell you, "Abortion is the only way to save the mother's life," you know they're misguided. Abortion does not directly solve or cure any woman's health problem.

Unintentional Death of the Child

That said, there are situations where the best solution for the mother's health might result, *unintentionally*, in the death of the unborn child. For example, take an ectopic pregnancy. In a healthy pregnancy, the fertilized egg attaches itself to the uterus and develops normally. But in an ectopic pregnancy, which happens in about 2 percent of pregnancies, the embryo gets stuck on its way to the uterus, and it begins to grow outside the uterus, usually in the fallopian tube. But the embryo can't survive in the fallopian tube. Worse, if the embryo is left there without treatment, it can also cause life-threatening bleeding for the mother and, in some cases, death. This is clearly a case where the mother's life may be in danger.

In most ectopic pregnancies, doctors decide to cut away the section of the fallopian tube where the embryo attached. This, of course, results in the death of the unborn child, but it saves the life of the mother and prevents further complications. Some people are surprised to learn that the Catholic Church actually permits this sort of procedure. How can that be? Isn't the doctor performing an abortion? Isn't he basically killing the child?

The answer has to do with a moral principle known as "double effect." The principle of double effect says an action can have two effects: one good effect that you intend and one bad effect that you foresee but *don't* intend. In the example of an ectopic pregnancy, the goal is to save the life of the mother and to heal her dysfunctional reproductive system. That's the intended good effect. To do that, a section of the fallopian tube must be removed, which is not intrinsically wrong.

But there's also a second, bad effect. The unborn child attached to that fallopian tube will die as a result of the procedure. That bad effect was foreseen—the doctors and the mother knew it would happen—but it was not intended. The doctor's goal was only to save the mother's life. If there was a way to save the mother's life *without* killing the unborn child, they would have gladly taken that option, but usually in an ectopic pregnancy, that option doesn't exist.

Therefore in this scenario, what was done was *not* an abortion, since abortion, remember, is the *direct, intentional* killing of an unborn child. In this case, though, the death of the child was indirect. It was the unintentional result of another procedure aimed at saving the mother's life. These distinctions are important, and they show how the Church can oppose abortion but at the same time allow for medical interventions that save a mother's life, even if those interventions unintentionally result in the death of an unborn child. The distinctions are subtle, but as with most serious moral questions, the subtleties carry a load of importance.

Let's recap briefly. In discussing the hard cases, your first move should be to determine whether the person is genuinely concerned about them or if they're just using the hard cases as a smokescreen. If you determine it's the former, you now have ways to talk about each situation.

ANSWERING THE BEST PRO-CHOICE OBJECTIONS

We've already handled many pro-choice arguments above, but let's consider some more of the top challenges you'll hear.

Objection 1: "A woman should decide what she does with her body. Nobody should tell her how to choose."

On the face of it, this sounds obvious: our bodies don't belong to anyone else. So nobody should tell us what to do with them. However, this argument assumes that abortion involves only one body: the mother's. But abortion always affects another body too. Scientists universally agree that the fetus is a distinct, living organism. It has unique human DNA, different from that of its mother. In other words, it's a unique human body. During pregnancy, the fetus is attached to the mother and depends on the mother for its development, but it's definitely not *part of her body*. It's a different, unique body *within* her body.

So what you want to communicate is that abortion doesn't involve just one body. It involves two bodies, the mother's and the unborn child's. Although we can agree that, in most cases, a woman can decide what she does with *her* body, we just can't agree she can do whatever she wants with *somebody else*'s body—namely, the body of the unborn child.

Objection 2: "Many of these kids will be born into poverty or abusive households. Their lives will be miserable. How could you force them into such a world?"

The best response to this argument is the "trot out the toddler" strategy. Millions of toddlers exist *right now* in awful situations, whether in terrible poverty, abusive families, or with little hope of advancement. Since their lives are miserable, should we just kill them? Well, of course not. No sensible person would choose that option. But if we wouldn't kill them, we shouldn't kill poor unborn children either.

In fact, we have an even stronger reason not to kill unborn children, since they only *potentially* will be raised in bad situations, while many born children *already* live under wretched conditions.

So whether someone is a fetus, a toddler, or an elderly person, and the person is facing miserable conditions, killing the person is never a good solution.

Objection 3: "We need abortion because otherwise we won't be able to care for all these children when the world is overpopulated."

The fact is, overpopulation is a myth. If you want the full scoop, and all the data, visit the website OverpopulationIsAMyth.com. But in the Western world—America, Canada, and much of Europe—we're not facing overpopulation but rather *underpopulation*.

Birth rates in America are the lowest that have ever been recorded. We're simply not replacing our population. Instead, we're shrinking. Sociologists tell us the optimal replacement rate to keep the population steady is 2.1 births per woman between the ages of fifteen and forty-four. But America averages 1.8 births per woman. In others words, we're not having enough babies to replace those who are dying. So abortion is a solution to a problem that doesn't exist. We need *more* babies, not fewer.

But suppose, for the sake of argument, that overpopulation was a serious threat. How should you respond? Well, here's a strategy adapted from Trent Horn's book *Persuasive Pro-Life*. He recommends saying to the objector,

> You know, when it comes to population dynamics, there are two types of people—givers and takers. The givers include people like scientists or political leaders who contribute knowledge or ingenuity that could help us solve the overpopulation problem. They help us grow food more efficiently or create affordable housing for more people. But then you have the takers. These include people such as the homeless, the severely disabled, or people in prison. In most cases, these people consume far more resources than they contribute. If that's the case and overpopulation is a serious threat, shouldn't we kill all the homeless, the severely disabled, prisoners, and others

who only consume resources and give nothing back? Then only after we've killed them
all, we can reassess and decide if we also need
to kill the unborn, since the unborn are innocent and could grow up to be either givers or
takers—we just don't know yet.[2]

Now, hopefully, the person will say, "No, of course we shouldn't kill the homeless, the sick, and those in prison just to ease overpopulation." Yet if they say that, they have even less reason to kill the unborn to prevent overpopulation.

Objection 4: "Stop trying to force your moral or religious views on everyone else!"

First, let's be clear that opposing abortion is not a religious issue. Do not let pro-choice people shut you down by writing you off as a religious extremist. Declare to your conversationalist that your pro-life views are not dependent on your religious beliefs. Affirm that you would stand against the killing of unborn children even if you weren't religious. In fact, while it's true that many religious groups oppose abortion, there are millions of *nonreligious* pro-life supporters too, including Secular Pro-Life, a large and growing movement of atheists and agnostics.

Also, notice how none of the arguments or tactics in this chapter rely on the Bible or other religious beliefs. Abortion is not fundamentally a religious issue. It's a moral issue that all people of goodwill can agree on. So be strong and don't let people dismiss your pro-life views on the basis of religion. Affirm that you're not using religion to support your views, and if they disagree, ask them to show you exactly how your arguments are based in religion.

But what about people who think you shouldn't force your particular moral views on everyone else? What if they say, "Well, I'm personally opposed to abortion, but I wouldn't force that view on everyone. Who am I to tell other people what to do with their own bodies?"

You can explain that enforcing moral views is exactly what democratic law is supposed to do. On any particular issue it takes one perspective or view, enshrines it in law, and expects everyone to follow it—even those who disagree with it. That's how our legal system works. So it's not wrong to promote your view or try to get it enshrined in law. After all, that's precisely what pro-choice advocates want to do! They want the law to reflect their pro-choice view. They want the law to allow for abortion.

Every law imposes some particular moral view on everyone, so it's important that we reflect on which laws are actually just and which laws we should promote. A democracy only works when people stand behind their views, offer evidence and support, and try to convince others to agree. That's the very heart of democracy. So, this just isn't a good objection.

Objection 5: "How does legalized abortion affect you? If you don't like abortions, just don't have one!"

In response you might offer an analogy: "Suppose you and I were having this discussion in the mid-1800s, and I said to you, 'How does legalized slavery affect you? If you don't like enslaving people, just don't have slaves!' I doubt you would accept that line of reasoning. You would agree that slavery is wrong and inhumane, and nobody should be enslaved. But the same principle applies to abortion. Abortion is wrong and inhumane, and nobody should be killed in the mother's womb. So it's not enough just for me not to have slaves, or just for me not to abort my own children. Slavery and abortion should be illegal for everyone, everywhere, because no human should have to suffer those atrocities."

Objection 6: "You're just a man, so you can't possibly understand the issue of abortion. You have no right to speak about it."

Men commonly hear this objection. Once again, the best response is an analogy.

You can say, "You're right, I've never had an abortion, so I can't speak from experience. I don't know the pain and struggle involved with that decision. But that doesn't prevent me from having an informed opinion about it. I've never experienced rape or murder or embezzlement, but I can say with confidence that those things are also definitely wrong. Similarly, most doctors haven't experienced

95 percent of the problems they seek to cure, but they're still able to make judgments and take action. I think any person can objectively look at the facts about abortion and come to the realization that it's wrong, regardless of whether they're male or female, or whether they've had an abortion themselves."

So now we have covered what to say about abortion and how to answer the best objections. Next let's consider some effective ways to communicate these truths.

TIPS AND STRATEGIES FOR DISCUSSING ABORTION

Tip 1: Always find common ground.

This is a great strategy for any hot-button topic, but it's especially useful with abortion. Because abortion is such an emotionally heated topic, you always want to look for shared principles or points on which you can agree with the other person. Then from there, you can jump into disagreements. You can find common ground by asking good questions such as these, which are from Trent Horn's helpful book, *Persuasive Pro-Life*. I've found them to be really effective in conversation:

Question 1: "What do you think about late-term abortions?" Get them to agree that at least some abortions are bad, especially those in the final months of pregnancy. And when they admit that, you can probe and ask why. You might say, "If you think they should be illegal, then where would you draw the line? Why did you pick that stage to outlaw abortions?"

Question 2: "What do you think about aborting a fetus simply because she is female?" Most people are against sex-selective abortions. So, if you get them to agree on that, then you have come to an understanding that you both are against *some* abortions. Then ask why sex-selective abortions are wrong.

Question 3: "Would you prefer there were fewer abortions?" Most people would say yes. In fact, I don't know anyone who actually thinks we need *more* abortions. But why? What is it about abortion they find unpleasant? Pro-choice supporters, including many politicians, claim abortions should be "safe, legal, and rare." But why rare? Again, what's wrong with abortion that makes us want to reduce the number of abortions? Find common ground by saying, "I agree we need fewer abortions," and then use that agreement to explore the question "Yet why fewer?"

Question 4: "Should abortion be legal through all nine months of pregnancy, for any reason?" If they respond that it should not, ask, "Why not? Where do you think the cutoff should be, and why do you draw the line *there*?"

The goal of these questions is not to make the other person look silly or evil but to find common ground. You want to see where you can both agree and then detect the shared principles that undergird that agreement.

For example, if you and a pro-choicer both agree that late-term abortions are wrong, that it's wrong to kill a child five minutes before the child is born, then you can explore together to determine *why* that's wrong. Hopefully the conversation will lead the other person to agree that it's wrong because the child is just as human five minutes *before* birth as five minutes *afterward*, and therefore we shouldn't kill the child.

Tip 2: Acknowledge the other person's good intentions.

It's tempting when talking about something as awful as abortion to see a pro-choice supporter as evil. After all, they support a practice that kills an innocent, unborn human child. But most abortion advocates are not willfully evil. They're not malevolent. They're just deeply misguided and confused. In fact, many of them think they're choosing the most compassionate, fair position.

If you want to have a productive dialogue, and potentially change their mind about abortion, you can't approach them in an accusatory or belittling way. Instead, first you want to acknowledge that they have good intentions. You might say something like, "Look, I think we can both agree that abortion is really emotional and complicated, and each woman's experience is different. I think you have a good heart and you're trying to do what's best for people, especially women. I really admire that."

By affirming the other person's good intentions, you'll make it far more likely that they'll listen to what you have to say. Then you can move forward by saying something like, "But wouldn't you agree that sometimes people with good intentions can be confused about what they choose?

You see where I'm coming from here? Don't you think it's possible that even if both of us are trying to do good and be compassionate, we may be confused about our beliefs?"

Your goal here is to affirm both that the other person's heart is in the right place and that their mind might be misguided, despite their good heart. This may not seem like a big deal, but when you start a conversation by acknowledging their good intentions, you'll be in a much better position to win them over.

Tip 3: Keep emphasizing equality.

Equality is a strong buzz word in our culture. Everyone, especially progressive political groups, champions equal rights. They want equal rights for same-sex couples, equal rights for transgender people, and equal rights for migrants, refugees, and racial minorities. So, when discussing abortion, channel that passion to support equal rights for the unborn.

You can say, "I think everyone should be treated equally, no matter how big or small, young or old. All humans should have an equal right to life. Don't you agree we should treat all humans equally?" For example, you might say, "I think we should treat the unborn with the same care we give other human beings. We should not isolate one class of people, especially an innocent, vulnerable minority like the unborn, and say, 'You don't get any rights.'"

Your goal here is to get these other people to choose. They have three options: Either they agree with you that all people, including the unborn, have the same right to life, which would be consistent with their passion for equality. Or they must acknowledge they don't want to give equal rights to this group of humans. Or they must deny that the unborn are humans at all. But whichever of those three options they choose, you'll know how to proceed based on the strategies in this chapter.

If they choose the first one, you've convinced them to protect unborn life. Mission accomplished! If they choose the second one, though, which claims the unborn don't deserve the right to life, you can press them on that position. Ask why, if the unborn are human, they deserve fewer rights than other humans. You can use the "trot out the toddler" strategy to do this. If they choose the third path, denying that the unborn are human at all, then use the supporting arguments for the one key question to show how they're just as human as the rest of us.

So those are three very effective strategies for discussing abortion: find common ground, acknowledge the other person's good intentions, and keep emphasizing equality. Use them, and I promise your conversations will be more fruitful and productive.

RECOMMENDED BOOKS
(in order of importance)

Trent Horn, *Persuasive Pro-Life: How to Talk about Our Culture's Toughest Issue* (Catholic Answers, 2014).

> A comprehensive collection of the best tips and strategies for discussing abortion with pro-choice advocates.

Gives wise answers to all the major arguments. Includes fictional dialogues that show Horn's tips and strategies being used in action.

Peter Kreeft, *Three Approaches to Abortion: A Thoughtful and Compassionate Guide to Today's Most Controversial Issue* (Ignatius Press, 2002).

A reflection on the objective logical arguments against abortion (the impersonal approach); the subjective, personal motives of the pro-life position (the personal approach); and how these two factors influence the dialogue between the two sides of the abortion issue (the interpersonal approach). A book with a respectful tone that you can pass on to friends who support abortion.

Scott Kluesendorf, *Pro-Life 101: A Step-by-Step Guide to Making Your Case Persuasively* (Stand to Reason Press, 2002).

A short, punchy, easy-to-read book about effective conversations with abortion activists. Includes a chapter on helping a friend through a crisis pregnancy.

Robert George and Christopher Tollefsen, *Embryo: A Defense of Human Life* (Doubleday, 2008).

Using rigorous science and philosophy, the authors make a compelling case that the unborn, even as embryos, are decidedly human and that it's just as wrong to kill an embryo as it is to kill a born human being.

Peter Kreeft, *The Unaborted Socrates: A Dramatic Debate on the Issues Surrounding Abortion* (InterVarsity Press, 1983).

An entertaining series of three dialogues: Socrates and an abortionist in an abortion clinic, Socrates and an ethicist at a philosophy convention, and Socrates and a psychologist in a psychiatric ward. Together, they represent the three most common angles from which people approach the abortion debate—the medical, the moral, and the psychological.

FOR REFLECTION AND DISCUSSION

1. What are the three main types of abortion? Describe each of them.
2. Why do you think the question "Are the unborn human?" works so effectively in conversations with abortion advocates?
3. What are some ways of convincing others that the unborn are human?
4. Why does the "trot out the toddler" strategy work so well to persuade people that abortion is always wrong?
5. What might you say to someone who holds that the unborn are not human because they depend completely on another person for their life?
6. How can you determine if a person's concern for the hard cases is genuine or a smokescreen?
7. In your opinion, which is the strongest pro-choice objection to the pro-life position on abortion? Why? How would you respond to it?

FOR PRACTICE

For each of the following scenarios, write a response using what you learned in this chapter. Follow the directions in parentheses.

1. A friend justifies abortion saying, "I know women who have had abortions, and you don't know what it's like. They're scared and their whole life has turned upside down. They don't have a choice. They don't have a job and they can't possibly support a new child. You're really going to force women into poverty." (Respond to the friend by trotting out the toddler.)

2. You are having a conversation with a cousin about abortion. She says that she can't understand why you oppose abortion. She approves of abortion for any reason, claiming that the fetus is just a blob of tissue and is not at all developed. (Respond to the cousin with the SLED analogy.)

6

SAME-SEX MARRIAGE

Have you ever been in a discussion about marriage and not known how to explain it without resorting to, "Well, that's just what I personally believe" or "That's just what the Church teaches"? Have you been in a tense discussion with family about marriage politics or who should be allowed to marry? Or have you yourself ever wondered what marriage is and why it matters?

I've discussed nearly every hot-button issue with friends and family. We've talked about abortion, war, politics, contraception, the pope, Jesus, you name it. But the one topic that seems to provoke the most tension and awkwardness is same-sex marriage.

You may have experienced the same thing. I'm guessing that if I showed you a list of difficult topics, the one you would feel least excited to discuss would be same-sex marriage. You're worried about being labeled a bigot or a hater. Although you know marriage is only between a man and a woman, you're just not sure how to defend that view while being sensitive and compassionate toward same-sex attracted people.

I promise that this chapter will help you to stop feeling that way. In these pages you'll come to understand the marriage issue inside and out. You'll have clarity on same-sex marriage and know how to discuss it calmly and charitably.

TODAY'S MOST CONTROVERSIAL ISSUE

Twenty-five years ago, same-sex marriage was on few people's radar. But throughout the early and mid-1990s, a growing group of same-sex couples began seeking marriage. They knew that the government incentivizes marriage. It wants people to get married, and it encourages marriages to remain intact. That's why it offers tax breaks, insurance benefits, social security, and other special perks to married couples.

Unsurprisingly, same-sex couples wanted these benefits too. They also wanted public recognition of their relationship. At the time, almost all the states defined marriage as the union of one man and one woman. But a few liberal states adjusted their definition to include same-sex couples, suddenly making our country's marriage policy a mixed bag. To add more confusion, there was no explicit definition of marriage from a federal perspective, so it became messy fast.

That all changed in 1996 when Congress passed the Defense of Marriage Act, also known as DOMA. For federal purposes this law defined marriage as the union of one man and one woman. States were still free to recognize same-sex relationships if they wanted, but those couples would not receive federal marriage benefits.

DOMA was relatively uncontroversial at the time. It passed by overwhelming majorities in both houses of Congress and was signed into law by the Democrat president, Bill Clinton. So as recently as a twenty years ago, marriage was understood by the large majority of people, citizens and politicians alike, as the union of one man and one woman.

Oh, how quickly things changed! Within a few years, the push for same-sex marriage took off in staggering ways. It gained the support of celebrities, TV writers, movies, and the media. Same-sex-attracted people came out of the closet. Many of us discovered we had friends or family members attracted to people of the same sex, which gave the issue flesh and bones. For growing numbers, it was no longer just a political discussion; it was a personal one.

By early 2016, thirty-six states were issuing marriage licenses to same-sex couples. It's worth noting that it was in only a few of these states that the people voted to allow same-sex marriage. In the majority of states, a small group of unelected judges imposed same-sex marriage on the people, often against the wishes of voters.

Then, in June 2016, the biggest ball dropped. The Supreme Court, in its landmark decision, *Obergefell v. Hodges*, overturned the Defense of Marriage Act. *Obergefell* claimed that the Constitution guarantees a fundamental right to marriage to all people, including same-sex couples. As a result, all states had to begin immediately issuing marriage licenses to same-sex couples and recognize all same-sex marriages performed across state lines. In one fell swoop, the Supreme Court legalized same-sex marriage in all fifty states.

This decision didn't come out of nowhere, though. The Supreme Court aligned with popular opinion. Consider these shocking statistics: Just fifteen years ago, 60 percent of Americans opposed same-sex marriage and only 31 percent supported it. But today, those numbers have flipped. A recent poll shows that 61 percent of Americans now *support* same-sex marriage while only 31 percent oppose it.[1] Among Millennials, those in their twenties and thirties, support for same-sex marriage has climbed to 74 percent. Support for same-sex marriage is at an all-time high.

What does all this mean for Catholics and others who support traditional marriage? Well, the cultural pressure is mounting. We all feel it. We sense the tension and disapproval whenever someone detects that we support traditional marriage. We're worried how people will react.

We see it in bigger ways too. For example, in April 2014, Brendon Eich, the CEO of Mozilla, the not-for-profit behind the Firefox browser, was pressured to resign because he had donated $1,000 to support a California pro-marriage law six years previously. A few employees at Mozilla learned about his donation and launched a campaign to oust Eich. And that happened even though he was on record as respecting the rights and dignity of gay employees at Mozilla. As a consequence, Eich lost his job. We've seen numerous other examples of bakers, florists, and restaurants that were badmouthed, sued, and destroyed because their conscience would not allow them to cater same-sex wedding ceremonies.

We don't know what the future might bring. But we do know that if we're to make any progress and clear up the massive confusion surrounding marriage, we need to do two things: first, we need to make a strong, clear case for traditional marriage, and second, we need to do it in an articulate, charitable way.

WHAT IS MARRIAGE?

What if I told you that the debate about same-sex marriage has nothing to do with homosexuality? That it has nothing to do with equality, bigotry, love, or any of the buzzwords often thrown around? The truth is that the same-sex-marriage debate is only about one thing—the definition of marriage. In other words, at root it's about our answer to this question: What is marriage?

Unfortunately, some people frame this as a debate about equality. You see "equal" signs on Facebook profiles and on bumper stickers. Same-sex marriage supporters claim their cause is about "marriage equality." They say they want same-sex attracted people to have equal access to marriage.

The problem is, we all support marriage equality. The person who supports traditional marriage believes in marriage equality just as much as the person who endorses same-sex marriage. We all want people to have equal access to marriage. We all believe marriage law should be equally applied.

What we differ on is that fundamental question: What is marriage? Before determining whether we're for or against marriage equality, we first have to nail down what we mean by "marriage." In today's world, there are two main answers to that question resulting in two different views of marriage. The first is the *conjugal* view of marriage, and the second is the *revisionist* view. The debate about same-sex marriage is really about which of these two visions is correct, so let's look at each of them.

The Conjugal View

What is the conjugal view of marriage? This view says that marriage is the institution that unites a man and a woman to each other and to any children born from their union. That definition is so important. In fact, I strongly advise you to memorize it.

Some people call this the traditional or historical understanding of marriage, but those terms can connote something dusty and outdated, so I prefer "conjugal view." On the conjugal view, marriage is fulfilled, or consummated, by what's known as the "conjugal act," and that's where it gets its name. The conjugal act is sexual intercourse, the act by which a man and a woman coordinate their whole selves toward a shared end—namely, unity and procreation. It is comprehensive because it involves the whole of two people—bodies, minds, and hearts—both uniting toward a single goal. In fact, the sexual act is the only biological act that requires two people to complete. Every other biological function we can do on our own. But the conjugal act requires two people. The conjugal act sometimes results in children, but not always. Yet it always unifies the spouses in a special way.

So again, marriage is the comprehensive union of a man and a woman oriented toward children. This view of marriage has been held by the overwhelming majority of people throughout history and by people living today. Notice that nowhere in that definition do we find religious terms. The conjugal view isn't just a Catholic or religious view. True, all of the world's major religions have historically understood marriage in this way, but this just means that no single religion invented marriage. Instead, almost all religions have arrived at the same obvious fact. The contours of marriage can be discerned by human reason alone, whatever our religious background, which is why many of the brightest pagan thinkers such as Socrates, Plato, Aristotle, Plutarch, and others understood marriage in the conjugal sense.

The Revisionist View

The revisionist view, on the other hand, tries to alter the conjugal view, redefining marriage to be the public recognition of a committed relationship between two adults, meant for their own fulfillment. In this view, marriage has no special connection to children or procreation. Marriage is just an intense emotional bond that is primarily about romance, love, and mutual affection. It's a couple-centered vehicle for personal growth and emotional intimacy.

In the revisionist understanding, marriage is similar to other types of relationships, just more intense. Or as the leading same-sex-marriage advocate John Corvino says, marriage is the relationship you have with your "number-one person." And since marriage is mainly about personal fulfillment, it's up to the partners to decide whether to have kids, whether to be sexually exclusive, or how long the marriage lasts. The marriage relationship can be adjusted, or even ended, when it stops fulfilling either partner.

So to recap what we've learned so far, the same-sex-marriage debate is really about one question: What is marriage? We have two main views to choose from: the conjugal view and the revisionist view. If the conjugal view is correct, then it's easy to see why marriage can only involve one man and one woman. That's the only relationship that can participate in a comprehensive union, and it's the only type of union capable of producing children.

But if the revisionist view is correct, and marriage is just about adult fulfillment, then practically *any* relationship can be recognized as a marriage. You could have a man and a woman, two men, two women, three people, a large group—it doesn't matter. If the revisionist view is correct, then people would be wrong to deny same-sex couples access to marriage.

Although the revisionist view is problematic, it's extremely popular today. It's the one championed in movies, media, books, TV, and even our schools. Thus it's not surprising that so many people support same-sex marriage today. They've accepted, often uncritically, the revisionist view that marriage is simply about mutual adult fulfillment.

When we talk about recognizing same-sex marriage, what we're really discussing is whether we should redefine marriage from the institution that unites a man and a woman to each other and to any children they produce, to the public recognition of a committed relationship for adults. Again, this isn't about homosexuality. It's not about rights, or equality, or even love. It's about the question that lies under all those considerations, the one we have to answer first: What is marriage?

Now that we've looked at the definition of marriage, though, let's turn to a natural follow-up question: Why does marriage matter?

WHY MARRIAGE MATTERS

Why does marriage matter in the first place? Why doesn't the government just ignore the question and get out of the marriage business altogether? Then we could avoid the whole same-sex marriage controversy. Everyone could just live and love as they please.

Many people lean this way today. After college, I worked for five years as a mechanical engineer, and I remember a chat I had with a coworker. We were both in our midtwenties, and we had both been in a relationship for six years. While I had been married to my wife for three of those years, and had two children, my friend was not married and marriage was nowhere on his horizon. I asked if he thought he would ever propose to his girlfriend, and his answer surprised me. He said, "You know, I'm just not sure. I love her, but my parents got divorced and it was really ugly. I have friends who married young and are already divorced. I'm just terrified of putting my girlfriend through that. I guess I just have a really low view of marriage. I don't see the point of it." He was essentially asking this question: What's the point of marriage? Why does it matter?

Why the Government Cares about Marriage

Clearly, the government thinks marriage matters. The government spends a lot of time and energy regulating marriage. It sets up marriage laws, it tells us whom we can and cannot marry, and it rewards those who get married. It even punishes people who violate marriage laws. But why? Have you ever thought about why the government cares so much about marriage? Why doesn't it legislate other types of relationships the way it legislates marriage? For example, the government doesn't legislate friendships. It doesn't tell you whom you can and cannot be friends with. You don't have to file for a "friendship" license in order to have your friendships legally recognized. Similarly, the government doesn't legislate sports teams, telling you whom you can or cannot play basketball with.

Presumably, the government isn't interested in our love lives, whom we prefer to have sex with, or what our most intense romantic relationship is. But the government *does* care about marriage. It makes laws about marriage, it offers special marriage benefits, and it tries to promote a healthy marriage culture. Why? The main reason is children. The government cares about marriage because it cares about children.

Society depends on children. In order to continue, society needs healthy, productive, new generations. The government makes laws about marriage to ensure that children are united to their mother and father, wherever possible, which gives them the best chance for success in life.

Specifically, being in the marriage business helps children in two ways: First, it ensures kids are raised by the mother and father who created them. Every child longs to know his mother and father and, where possible, to be raised by them. Marriage cements that bond.

Second, marriage is the best way to ensure parents stick together, even during tough times. With other relationships, it's fine to have temporary bonds. For instance, I might join a soccer team for a few months, but it's not a huge deal if I move and have to quit the team. But with the marriage relationship, permanence matters. Ideally, men and women need to stick together for the sake of children. Without marriage, sexual relationships tend to become temporary. Fathers are especially likely to leave, forcing mothers to raise children on their own. Obviously, this is not good for women or their children. A child needs both parents, not just one or the other.

To recap briefly, marriage matters because it's the only institution that unites a man and a woman to each other and to any children they create. And the government promotes marriage, regulates it, and offers incentives to those who get married because it cares about the welfare of children.

THREE MARRIAGE FACTS

We now understand what marriage is, and why it matters, but how do we affirm the conjugal view over the revisionist view? The best approach is to identify some common facts about marriage that people on both sides agree with. And then we can ask, "Which view of marriage best explains those facts?" I love this approach because it starts on common ground. When chatting with a friend, you can say, "OK. You believe marriage is one thing, and I think it's another. But both of us agree that marriage has these features—A, B, and C. Which of our two views best accounts for these features?"

Experts sometimes call these features "marital norms," elements that are normal and necessary for all true marriages. The three norms we'll look at are permanence, fidelity, and monogamy. Almost everyone accepts these three norms whether they're for or against same-sex marriage, for or against redefining marriage.

Permanence

Most of us agree that marriage is for life. When you marry someone, you commit to stay together "until death do us part." Of course, we all know divorce is rampant and many marriages fall apart. But we usually don't highlight divorces as good. Divorce suggests something split that was intended to remain whole. For example, we talk about "broken marriages." We use this sort of language because we know, intuitively, that marriage is supposed to be permanent. Even if we sometimes fail to live up to that ideal, that's the natural goal of marriage.

But if marriage is meant to be permanent, which of the two visions of marriage best accounts for this ideal? On the conjugal view, it's easy to see the importance of permanence. If marriage is about uniting two spouses so they can create and raise children, permanence is crucial. Children need stability, and spouses need the assurance that their partner is in it until the end, that they're not going to back out when things get tough.

But on the revisionist view, marriage is just an intense emotional or romantic bond and has no special connection to kids. As we all know, especially those of us who have been married for several years, romantic feelings ebb and flow. If the revisionist view is right, and that's all marriage is, then why stay married when the feelings go away? The revisionist view gives no reason to think marriage must be permanent. Sure, some spouses may choose to stick together for life, but they're doing so out of preference, not out of principle. And the preference could change.

So only the *conjugal* view makes sense of the fact that marriage should be permanent.

Fidelity

Fidelity means faithfulness, specifically sexual faithfulness. When two people get married, they almost always pledge, whether explicitly or implicitly, to be sexually faithful to each other. If you want proof of this, just look at how hurt and betrayed people feel when they discover their partner has been sleeping around. This is true for almost all couples, even same-sex couples.

We know that's not how marriage is meant to work. Marriage is supposed to be sexually exclusive. You pledge only to share sexual union with your spouse and nobody else. Yet if sexual fidelity is a marital norm, which view accounts best for it?

On the conjugal view, faithfulness makes sense. Since marriage is about uniting to create and raise children, it's evident that we should commit sexually to only one spouse. If married people slept around, they would not only risk having children with different partners, partners they're not fully committed to, but also destroy their original relationship with their spouse, and that would create a whirlwind of problems for their children. Sexual fidelity ensures that spouses only have children with each other, within the bond of marriage.

But on the revisionist view, why is fidelity important? If marriage is essentially about personal fulfillment, what's wrong with spouses sleeping around if that's what fulfills them? Thankfully, most couples who adopt the revisionist approach don't sleep around. And that's a good thing. But they have no principled reason to remain faithful other than personal preference. In other words, they're faithful *in spite of* their view of marriage, not because of it. If marriage is primarily an intense sexual relationship, there's no reason it must be exclusive. Only the conjugal view can account for sexual fidelity.

Monogamy

Monogamy refers to the fact that married people have only one spouse. Although other romantic relationships are on the rise, such as polygamy, which involves one man and multiple wives, and polyamory, which involves multiple men and multiple wives, most people agree they should not be recognized as marriages. Even the majority of those who support same-sex marriage think marriage should only involve two people.

On the conjugal view, marriage can only be between one man and one woman because only that pair can unite sexually in the type of act that produces children. Therefore, marriage ties someone to only one partner. Multiple partners can't share a conjugal, or comprehensive, union.

But on the revisionist view, since marriage has no special connection to procreation and is merely an intense romantic or sexual bond, there's no good reason to limit it to two people. Why can't three or more people share an intense bond? The revisionist view offers no good answer.

To be clear, we are not saying that people holding the revisionist view are incapable of sharing permanent, faithful, monogamous relationships. Most do. We're just saying that when such relationships bear these traits, it's *despite* their view of marriage and not *because* of it.

So keep these three marital norms in mind—permanence, fidelity, and monogamy. Then when you find yourself discussing marriage, you can bring them up, saying, "Hey, let me ask you something. You agree that, ideally, marriage should be permanent, right? And that it should be faithful? That you shouldn't sleep around? And that you should only have one partner, not two, three, or four? Right? We both agree on all of that, so let's start there and ask, Which of our views about marriage best explains those facts?" This logic is a powerful way to help people see why the conjugal view of marriage makes the most sense.

Expert Interview with Ryan T. Anderson

➤ **Watch the interview here: https://claritasu.com/anderson**

Ryan Anderson is a senior research fellow at the Heritage Foundation and the founder and editor of the journal *Public Discourse*. He has published numerous articles in both scholarly journals and popular magazines. And he has published several books, including *What Is Marriage? Man and Woman: A Defense*, which he coauthored.

In this interview, Anderson responds to the following questions:

1. Why is the question "What is marriage?" so central and important?
2. What is your definition of marriage?
3. What is the "revisionist view" of marriage, and why is it misguided?
4. Many opponents of the traditional view say if marriage has a special link to children, then what about infertile or elderly couples? How do you answer this objection?
5. Why is it OK to allow interracial marriages but not OK to allow same-sex marriages?

6. How can I discuss same-sex marriage with sensitivity?
7. What are some talking points you might recommend for discussing the case for marriage?

Excerpt from the Interview

"To unite comprehensively with another person is going to be a union of hearts and minds and bodies. And to unite bodily with another person is to become one flesh. So, there's only one action that exists in which a man and a woman jointly perform a single action and it makes them into a one-flesh union." (Ryan T. Anderson)

RESPONDING TO SAME-SEX MARRIAGE SLOGANS

We've had a fairly comprehensive look at what marriage is and why it matters. But you might be thinking, "Yeah, that's really helpful, but how do I have fruitful conversations about same-sex marriage? How can I talk about it without coming across as bigoted or mean or just plain confused?" First, let's consider how to reply to the most common same-sex marriage slogans and one-liners. Then we'll focus on some very practical tips and strategies to move the conversation forward in the right direction.

Slogan 1: "If you reject same-sex marriage, you must be a bigot, homophobe, or hater."

How many times have you seen these labels tossed around? They're very common, especially in the media. Many assume that if you disagree with same-sex marriage, the only explanation is that you're a bigot, homophobe, or hater. If someone accuses you of this, you have two good options. You can either show that accusers are painting with too broad a brush, or you can defuse their accusations by defining the terms.

Too Broad a Brush

Ask questions challenging the accusations. You may say, "So if it's true that people who reject same-sex marriage must be bigots, homophobes, or haters, do you think President Bill Clinton was a bigot when he signed the Defense of Marriage Act into law? Or his wife, Senator Hilary Clinton, when she supported traditional marriage up until 2016? Or how about the millions of Americans who still support traditional marriage today? Do you really think *all of them* are bigots, homophobes, and haters?"

Most people would not be willing to go that far. Sure, *some* people who oppose same-sex marriage are bigots and haters, just as some people who oppose traditional marriage are bigots and haters. But it just doesn't follow that everyone who believes in traditional marriage must bear those labels. We can't paint with too broad a brush.

Define the Terms

A second way to handle these accusations is to define the actual terms. A bigot is someone who treats people with fear and intolerance. A homophobe is someone who doesn't like homosexuals or who is afraid of homosexuals. A hater is someone who intensely despises other people.

After defining those labels, you can then ask whomever you're talking with, "With those definitions in mind, do you really think those labels apply to me? I may disagree with same-sex marriage, but I have homosexual friends and I like them. I have no fear of homosexuals. I don't hate people with same-sex attraction. I'm not intolerant about whom they decide to love or be intimate with—that's their business. I just think the law should recognize the truth of marriage, which is a comprehensive union between a man and a woman. So how does that make me a bigot or hater?"

It's also helpful to point out that slinging around labels is usually an attempt to shut down the actual argument. It's a rhetorical tactic known as the *ad hominem* fallacy, which involves smearing a person's character or motivations to avoid engaging the person's beliefs. You can point this out by saying something like, "Look, those labels might be true, but how are they relevant to the discussion about what marriage is? If my view of marriage is wrong, it's wrong regardless of my personal motivations."

Slogan 2: "Look, we don't keep two people marrying because of race, so why sexual orientation?"

To respond to this, first you should admit that until the civil-rights movement, many state laws enforced racial segregation, which indeed prevented interracial couples from marrying. And we can all agree this was wrong. But you then want to make the point that it was wrong *because* race has nothing to do with marriage. Interracial couples can meet all the basic requirements of marriage. They can share a comprehensive union through the conjugal act. However, two men or two women can't enter this sort of relationship. That's not because their relationship is less intense or less valuable than others. It's because they can't share in the generative sexual act. While marriage must be color-blind, it can't be gender-blind.

You can marry someone of the opposite race, but you can't marry someone of the same gender. Therefore, the "race" objection is simply not a good one.

Slogan 3: "If marriage is about children, then what about infertile couples? Are you saying they're not really married?"

This objection tries to undermine the argument for traditional marriage by exposing a contradiction, but there's really no problem here. It's true that marriage is fundamentally about children and that it depends on the sexual act being ordered toward bearing children. So a couple is truly married if they share the conjugal act that is aimed at producing children, whether that act produces children or not.

Here's an analogy you can use in conversation. Consider this question: What distinguishes a baseball team from other groups of people? What makes a group of players a baseball team is that they are coordinated to the same end—winning baseball games. But if a baseball team plays a hundred games and doesn't win a single one, if they go zero for a hundred, are they still a baseball team? Of course. What matters is not whether they win any baseball games but the fact that they're collectively aimed at winning baseball games, which is what makes a baseball team a baseball team.

Similarly, as long as a couple can consummate their marriage by engaging in the conjugal act, then they're able to marry. This is why infertile couples are capable of marriage, but same-sex couples are not, because they can still engage in the conjugal act.

Slogan 4: "People have the right to love whomever they want. Love is love! Love wins!"

To deal with this popular slogan you just need to make two points. First, the same-sex-marriage debate is not about whom people can love. Everyone agrees that people have the right to love whomever they want.

But second, that doesn't mean all loving relationships should be classified as marriages. For instance, I love my sister, but I don't demand people call our relationship a marriage. I love my parish priest, but that doesn't mean we're married. When we're talking about marriage, what matters is not whether you love somebody or how strong that love is. What matters is whether you share a comprehensive sexual union with that person that tends to result in children.

Slogan 5: "You've already lost the debate. Get with the times! You're on the wrong side of history!"

It's true that the Supreme Court has made same-sex marriage legal in all fifty states and that popular support for it is quickly growing. If you hold to the traditional view, you're probably on the wrong side of the majority.

A Bigoted Appeal to Popularity

But just as with the labels of bigot, homophobe, and hater, this is an attempt to shut down dialogue. Ironically, the slogan is an example of bigotry—the very thing traditional marriage supporters get accused of. A bigot is one who refuses to consider a particular view or argument and just flippantly dismisses it.

You can respond by showing that the slogan is just an appeal to popularity. The exhortation "get with the times" says that since many people support same-sex marriage today, perhaps even the majority, you should too! But we don't accept this reasoning elsewhere. For example, would you say to an abolitionist in the year 1800, "Look, almost all people support slavery, so get with the times! Don't be on the wrong side of history!" We know that the majority might be wrong, as it has been many times in the past.

A Dwindling Minority

Second, you could compare the same-sex-marriage movement to the abortion-rights movement in the 1960s. After *Roe v. Wade* in 1973, which legalized abortion across the country, most people celebrated abortion. People believed that abortion on demand was a done deal. The people wanted it, the Supreme Court supported it, and those who disagreed were a dwindling minority. This held true for several decades.

But around fifteen years ago, things changed. Thanks to ultrasounds, better science, and pro-life activism, today the majority of people in America are pro-life. This is especially true of younger generations. It turns out that the dwindling minority who *opposed* abortion back in the 1960s were on the right side of history, even if few people knew it at the time.

Political victories are often temporary. Just as the abortion discussion did not end in 1973, we shouldn't think the same-sex-marriage debate is closed. We have barely passed a decade of serious conversation on the issue, the first of many to come. So there's no sense in telling people to "get with the times" or to "stand on the right side of history."

GETTING THE MARRIAGE CONVERSATION RIGHT

To the extent that same-sex-marriage advocates have won this debate, it has not been because their ideas are more persuasive. Their victory was achieved through slogans, label slinging, and appeals to emotion. This means that current victories for the same-sex-marriage movement are both fragile and reversible. Far too many of our neighbors haven't heard our arguments. They may find our position odd, but only because they don't understand what we believe. It's up to us to change that perception.

To do this we need to get the marriage conversation right. Let's consider some tips that will help you say the right things in the right way.

Tip 1: Always bring the discussion back to the main question: What is marriage?

If you take away just one thing from this chapter, it's that the same-sex marriage discussion is not really about homosexuality, love, equality, same-sex parenting, or any other side issues. It's about one thing: What is marriage? Until we settle that question, nothing else matters.

As we've seen, the marriage debate is a debate about two opposing answers to this question: the conjugal view and the revisionist view. The conjugal view says marriage is only between a man and a woman, while the revisionist view says any pairing or grouping can become a marriage. Accepting the revisionist view would change the definition of marriage.

So if someone asks you why you oppose same-sex marriage, say, "I don't oppose same-sex marriage. I oppose *redefining* marriage to something other than the union of one man and one woman." This will turn the discussion back to the right question.

Tip 2: Don't demean homosexual people or same-sex couples.

Explain that holding the traditional view of marriage does not mean you think homosexual people are evil or that their relationships are less loving or less valuable than other relationships. When you affirm this, you'll defuse a lot of tension in the conversation. You'll make it far more likely that your conversation partner will be open to what you're saying.

Also, conduct the dialogue with understanding and kindness. The *Catechism of the Catholic Church* directs us to accept same-sex attracted people with "respect, compassion and sensitivity" (*CCC*, 2358). And Jesus commands us to treat everyone with love, even those with whom we disagree.

Tip 3: Don't use "I believe" language.

When talking about the definition of marriage, don't say, "I believe marriage is between one man and one woman." For many people, the word *believe* implies this is your personal preference, the way "I believe" chocolate is better than vanilla or "I believe" the LA Lakers are the most exciting basketball team. Instead say, "Marriage *is* the institution that unites a man and a woman to each other and to any children they produce." That's a fact. It isn't your personal definition of marriage. It's what marriage *is* for everyone, in every place, at every time. You can speak so matter-of-factly because you're not discussing preferences; you are stating objective truths. So, don't say, "I believe marriage is . . .";

just say, "Marriage is . . ." Otherwise, you'll undercut your own case.

Tip 4: Affirm that marriage is about the needs of children, not the desires of adults.

The revisionist view of marriage wrongly holds that marriage is primarily about the personal fulfillment of two or more grown-ups, often at the peril of any children involved. To the contrary, you should keep driving home the point that marriage is fundamentally about children. Use the convincing fact that the government legislates about marriage because it is the only institution that unites children to their parents. Not all marriages produce children, but all children have a mom and a dad and deserve the chance to be raised by them whenever possible. That's why marriage exists; that's what marriage is about.

Tip 5: Emphasize that same-sex marriage does not "expand" marriage—it redefines it.

Many people who support same-sex marriage try to frame the conversation this way: "Why can't same-sex couples enter marriage just like other couples? They want to experience the goods of marriage too. So why can't we just expand the definition of marriage to include them?" When you phrase it this way, it sounds as if you're just making a minor adjustment to the essence of marriage; you're just stretching the borders a little bit.

But calling same-sex relationships "marriages" would not expand the institution of marriage. It would fundamentally redefine it, as we've seen. Pointing this out will refocus the conversation. Once everyone agrees that what's being pursued is a redefinition—a *new* definition of marriage, not an expansion—you can focus on discerning what the correct definition of marriage should be.

RECOMMENDED BOOKS
(in order of importance)

William May, *Getting the Marriage Conversation Right: A Guide for Effective Dialogue* (Emmaus Road, 2012).

This book shows you how to defend traditional marriage in nonreligious terms. In a popular, conversational style, May explores the origins, issues, and direction of the same-sex-marriage debate. He also includes a large and helpful FAQ section.

Sherif Gergis, Ryan T. Anderson, and Robert P. George, *What Is Marriage? Man and Woman: A Defense* (Encounter Books, 2012).

This book offers a philosophical defense of the reasons for the historic consensus that marriage is a male-female union. And it shows why redefining civil marriage is unnecessary, unreasonable, and contrary to the common good. *What Is Marriage?* has become extremely influential in the national culture.

Austen Ivereigh and Kathryn Lopez, *How to Defend the Faith without Raising Your Voice: Civil Responses to Catholic*

Hot-Button Issues (Our Sunday Visitor, 2015; be sure to get this edition).

Covers same-sex marriage and abortion, among other major concerns. The book takes the approach of first presenting the current cultural frame of the issue and then showing how to reframe it so it can be dealt with according to reason and truth.

Ryan T. Anderson, *Truth Overruled: The Future of Marriage and Religious Freedom* (Regnery, 2015).

A comprehensive study of the social reality of traditional marriage and same-sex marriage, assessing the present situation and projecting the future. Reflects on how the discussion of the marriage issues affects the fundamental rights of religious liberty.

FOR REFLECTION AND DISCUSSION

1. What accounts for the success of the same-sex-marriage movement?
2. Why is the same-sex-marriage debate only about one thing, the definition of marriage?
3. What are the main elements of the conjugal view of marriage? Of the revisionist view?
4. The book contends that the traditional view of marriage is not based on religion. How so?
5. Why is the government so interested in marriage?

6. Since a same-sex couple can conform to the three marital norms of permanence, fidelity, and monogamy, why can't they get married?

FOR PRACTICE

For each of the following scenarios, write a response using what you learned in this chapter.

1. People who say that two men can't get married are bigoted traditionalists. My two friends Harry and Jim are in love and want to marry. Why do you take such a hateful stance toward them?

2. I don't believe the government should be involved in marriage at all. They should be out of the marriage business altogether and let people make their own decisions.

3. You're on the wrong side of history with this one. I suggest you jump on board the marriage-equality side before you end up like the segregationists after the civil-rights era.

7

TRANSGENDERISM

I remember watching a viral YouTube video titled "Gender Identity," which sports more than three million views—I wasn't sure whether to laugh or weep.

Here's what happened. Recently, a five-foot-nine, white, male journalist visited the University of Washington. He walked around the campus and interviewed eight students, asking them questions about gender identity. But then the journalist asked the students what they would say if he told them he was a female. Every student said it would be OK.

But there's more. He next asked what if he identified as Chinese. The students were a bit more hesitant, but nobody denied him that label. One student said, "If you identified as Chinese, I might be a little surprised, but I would say, 'Good for you—be who you are.'" The journalist pushed a little more. He asked, "What if I told you I was seven years old?" Again, the students balked a little, but again, nobody offered resistance. One student said, "If you feel seven at heart, then so be it. Good for you!"

Finally, the five-foot-nine white guy asked, "What if I told you I was six foot five?" Would they affirm him? Thankfully, a couple of students admitted they'd say, "No, because you aren't really six foot five." But one student said,

"If you truly believe you're six foot five, I don't think it's harmful. I think it's fine if you believe that. I would not tell you you're wrong."

I still can't believe those responses. Although a few of the students were hesitant to affirm he was a six-foot-five, seven-year-old, Chinese female, they concluded it would be within his rights to identify however he pleases. One young woman summed up this attitude, saying, "I feel like that's not my place as another human to say someone is wrong or to draw lines or boundaries."[1]

Questions about identity have become a major battleground in the sexual/cultural arena, and many of us struggle to discuss it. Sometimes, we feel like those college students. We're confronted by someone, maybe even a person we love, such as a relative or friend, who identifies as something they're clearly not. We might think they are misguided, but what do we say? How should we respond?

In this chapter we're going to focus on the volatile and controversial topic of transgenderism. Transgenderism encompasses a host of issues revolving around men and women, males and females, sex and gender, and more. This chapter will help you understand the subject inside and out and show you how to discuss it with family, friends, and coworkers.

This is an important consideration. The "T" in LGBT activism is getting a lot louder. LGBT stands for lesbian, gay, bisexual, and transgender. After seeing sweeping victories in the LGB realm, activists are now turning to the T.

WHY TRANSGENDERISM MATTERS TO YOU

Transgenderism is everywhere. You can hardly get through the day without seeing a news story about it, whether a human-interest story about someone transitioning from one sex to another, about a male sports figure who has announced he's actually female, or about the politics of transgender rights or which restrooms transgendered persons should use.

Maybe it hasn't touched your life directly yet, and you just find the whole thing strange and off-putting. So why should you care about transgenderism at all?

Well, let's quickly tour through its landscape to see why. Today, there are five major areas where the transgender movement is pushing hard.

Mainstream Culture

Undoubtedly, the most prominent transgender story of our time concerns Bruce Jenner. Jenner was a former Olympian gold medalist. He appeared on Wheaties boxes and at one time was proclaimed the world's greatest athlete. He was a hero to many kids.

Yet in 2015, at age sixty-five, Jenner announced to the world in a *20/20* interview that his true identity was a woman. He underwent cosmetic and sex-reassignment surgeries. He changed his name to Caitlyn. Within a couple of months he appeared on the cover of *Vanity Fair* magazine with the headline, "Call me Caitlyn." Almost overnight,

Jenner became the world's most famous transgender figure, praised by nearly every media outlet. He was even honored by ESPN with its Arthur Ashe Courage award, given to especially brave sports figures.

But Jenner was only the beginning. Amazon Prime jacked up the momentum with a new television show called *Transparent* that portrays an older man who transitions to become a female. The program has won multiple Emmys and has been lauded by transgender advocates. The show advanced social and political activism through entertainment. Even its own writers talk about it with words like "propaganda," "agenda," and "seditious."[2]

In January 2017, *National Geographic* joined the bandwagon by placing a nine-year-old boy on the cover of their magazine, except the boy had pink hair, was dressed in girl clothes, and appeared behind a big title that said "Gender Revolution." The whole edition of *National Geographic* was dedicated to the topic of gender and transgenderism.

From TV to sports, magazines, and the internet, the mainstream culture is treating transgenderism with unequivocal and enthusiastic support.

The Restroom Controversies

Transgender activists argue that people who believe their gender is different than their biological sex should be free to use the bathroom that corresponds with their perceived gender. For example, a man who thinks he is female should be allowed to use the female bathroom. Predictably, these appeals have been met with resistance, especially from worried parents who don't want men sharing a bathroom with their young girls and from people who just feel uncomfortable using the restroom alongside members of the opposite sex.

One flashpoint here was the passing of North Carolina's 2016 bill titled HB2, which said all people must use restrooms that correspond with their biological sex. The law produced enormous outrage and was slammed for being hateful, bigoted, and discriminatory. Singers canceled events in North Carolina; the NBA pulled its All-Star Game out of Charlotte; and PayPal withdrew plans for a North Carolina expansion. These bathroom wars later hit Target and other retailers and remain a contentious battleground.

Schools

Transgenderism is also making waves in the classroom. Consider Nova Classical Academy, which is a K–12 charter school in St. Paul, Minnesota. Nova teaches a classical curriculum of grammar, logic, and rhetoric. *U.S. News and World Report* named it the number-one high school in Minnesota and the number-four charter high school in the country. In October 2015, parents of the elementary students at Nova received an email from the principal, informing them that in the coming year, the school would be supporting a five-year-old student "who is gender non-conforming." To support the gender-nonconforming child, all elementary students were required to read a book called *My Princess Boy* that "tells the story of a boy who expresses his true self by dressing up and enjoying traditional girl things."[3]

While all the parents agreed the kindergarten boy should be treated kindly, many believed that gender identity was an inappropriate classroom topic for five- to ten-year-olds. Parents who questioned the proposed changes were branded as bigots. Before this blowup, the school was a thriving educational institution where families of widely differing beliefs coexisted happily. Within a few months bitterness and distrust were rampant. Friendships had been destroyed, and a significant number of families left the school, which lost nearly a hundred students over the next year.

Also, it's worth noting that the father of the original transgender boy was a PhD candidate in psychology, doing research on "the creation and implementation of gender inclusive policies and practices in K–12 public schools." And even after Nova implemented a comprehensive gender-inclusion policy, the parents of the transgender boy withdrew him from the school. Then they sued Nova, objecting that the school informed parents they could opt their child out of instruction on transgender topics.

The Nova case isn't an isolated one. Transgenderism advocacy in the classroom is increasingly common. Through children's books and propaganda, often framed as antibullying activism, public schools across the country are teaching students that gender identity, sex, and gender expression are all free-floating concepts.

Hospitals

Many hospitals, including Catholic institutions, refuse to perform sex-reassignment surgeries, not just for religious and moral reasons, but because they're convinced these surgeries are dangerous, because they don't really solve the underlying problems, and because not nearly enough research has been conducted on them. Activists are increasingly accusing such hospitals of bigotry or of denying transgender people their right to surgery, or even, in their language, their right to "trans-affirming healthcare."[4]

In response, the US Department of Health and Human Services has begun compelling doctors to prescribe cross-sex hormones, even for young children, and to perform reassignment surgeries under the threat of hefty fines, closure of their facilities, or even imprisonment.

Pronouns

As long as the English language has existed, people have referred to a male person as "he" and a female person as "she." That will no longer be the case, if transgender supporters have their way. There are now dozens of proposed labels including "they," "per," "ve," and "ze." If you don't call a person by the pronoun he or she prefers, you are in danger of being accused of bigotry or even violence. Recently, a new bill introduced in California aimed to punish the "misgendering" of nursing-home patients. A worker who refused to call patients by their preferred pronouns would face fines of up to $1,000, jail time for up to a year, or both.

These five trends make it clear that we're living in very troubled, confused times. But this isn't all doom and gloom. It's actually a great opportunity. This confusion offers a chance to bring light and clarity to a darkening situation, and this chapter will show you how.

UNDERSTANDING TRANSGENDERISM

Key Terms

What is transgenderism? The first step to any good discussion is to define our terms, to make sure both people in the conversation understand the same words in the same way. There are five terms you really need to understand on this issue. They are *sex*, *gender*, *gender identity*, *gender dysphoria*, and *transgender*.

Sex

Sex refers to your biological makeup as either male or female. There are only two sexes—a scientific fact. Our genes determine which of those two sexes we are, and our biological sex can never change. It's hardwired by our DNA. Regardless of our appearances, our emotions, and our beliefs, we will always and only ever be either male or female.

Gender

Traditionally, *gender* has been attached to *sex* with reference to social and cultural differences. If your sex was male, you had a male or masculine gender. If your sex was female, you had a female or feminine gender. But today, many believe gender is disconnected from sex. You might be a biological male, they say, while having a female or feminine gender. But transgender advocates suggest there are more than just two genders. In fact, Facebook allows you to choose from more than fifty different possible genders when signing up for the service.

Gender Identity

This refers to an individual's self-perception of whether they are male or female, masculine or feminine. All of us have a gender identity. But while most people have a gender identity that matches their biological sex, some people feel their gender identity does not align with their sex.

Gender Dysphoria

Dysphoria is a psychological term for feelings of mental or emotional discomfort, confusion, and distress. *Gender dysphoria* refers to the distressing experience someone has when they sense a mismatch between their gender and their sex.

I want to emphasize that gender dysphoria is a real experience. There are really people who experience deep anguish and confusion because they feel trapped in the wrong body. It is, by most accounts, a horrible and unchosen condition. Few people who suffer from gender dysphoria are happy about it. After all, can you imagine how terrifying it would be to feel you've been trapped in the wrong body? Who would want that for themselves?

Gender dysphoria operates along a spectrum from mild to severe. Sometimes dysphoria is felt more intensely and demands resolution, and other times it's mild and manageable. Also, not all people who experience a mis-matched gender identity suffer from dysphoria. They might be totally happy and comfortable with the mismatch. But psychologists tell us the overwhelming majority of people with gender confusion *do* suffer from dysphoria.

Transgender

This is an umbrella term for the condition of identifying with or expressing a gender identity that does not match your sex. Transgenderism can take many forms, from a mental state to cross-dressing, hormonal treatment, and sex-reassignment surgery. *Transgender* can also refer to people who change their gender identity, which is known as being *gender fluid*. Or it can designate someone who identifies with a gender besides male or female, which is usually described as *nonbinary* or *agender*.

Statistics

How prevalent is transgenderism? It's estimated that around 0.3 percent of the American population identifies as transgender, or around seven hundred thousand people, but that number is growing fast. Some estimate it's as high as 1 to 2 percent today. We know that it's rising fastest among children and adolescents. Until a few years ago, most physicians and therapists estimated that less than 1 percent of children displayed gender confusion. But today that number has skyrocketed. As more schools and parents relentlessly affirm gender fluidity, the number of confused kids will continue to soar. There's no agreed-upon estimate, but some psychologists believe that upwards of 5 to 10 percent of children struggle with their gender identity.

According to the American Psychological Association, which is generally pro-transgender, roughly 70 to 80 percent of kids who report transgender feelings spontaneously lose those feelings over time. In other words, the huge majority of children grow out of their confusion. This is why it's problematic when doctors prescribe treatments for children that have permanent effects, things like hormone therapy or even sex-reassignment surgery. These treatments permanently fix disorders that the children otherwise likely would have grown out of, only now they can't, because surgery locked them in.

Here's another important statistic, one that should be distressing to all of us. According to the American Academy of Pediatrics, roughly 40 percent of transgender young people have attempted suicide. For many of them, feelings of confusion, despair, harassment, and rejection lead them to think life is no longer worth living. This is a major crisis that all of us, regardless of our views about transgenderism, need to lament and try to fix.

Some people suggest the way to curb these suicides is to increase medical interventions, such as hormonal therapy and sex-reassignment surgery. If we only allow transgender people to undergo surgery, they argue, the suicides would go down. But a prominent 2011 study in Sweden should give pause to that idea. The long-term study, which spanned more than thirty years and followed 324 people who had sex-reassignment surgery, revealed that after having sex-reassignment surgery, initially the transgender people had reduced rates of stress, dysphoria, and despair. But beginning about ten years later, transgendered people began to experience increasing mental difficulties. Most shockingly, their suicide rate rose almost twenty times above the comparable nontransgender population. The researchers pointed out that the higher suicide rate wasn't because such people still faced social pressure or rejection. Sweden is one of the most pro-transgender countries in the world. Yet still, transgendered people felt driven, in massive numbers, to commit suicide.

This means that for most people suffering from gender dysphoria, surgery isn't the cure. It doesn't treat the underlying problems. It doesn't address the discomfort of feeling you were born in the wrong body, and in many cases, it makes things worse. If nothing else, this data should caution us against prescribing surgery to anyone confused about their gender.

Finally, what causes gender dysphoria? Well, the true answer is we don't know. Studies of identical twins who share 100 percent of their DNA show it's not primarily a genetic issue. If people were born with a mismatched gender, we would expect all identical twins to share the same gender feelings. But they don't. In fact, the largest twin study shows that only 28 percent of identical twins both identify as transgender, despite their identical DNA. So it's not wholly dependent on your genetic makeup.

The research tells us the primary determinant factors occur after birth and are environmental. For instance, among children some of the primary causes of gender dysphoria include their being taught that gender fluidity is normal and being encouraged to experiment with their identity by family, teachers, or friends.

But regardless of what causes it, gender dysphoria is a very real phenomenon. Millions of people suffer profound distress over their gender identity.

THE CATHOLIC VIEW OF TRANSGENDERISM

How has the Catholic Church responded to transgenderism? Since the transgender movement is relatively new, there isn't an official Church document that focuses on transgenderism. But we do find it popping up in several encyclicals and papal quotes. Pope Francis, for example, has been repeatedly clear in his warnings about gender ideology, describing it as the "annihilation of man as the image of God."[5]

When the pope refers to man as the image of God, he's of course alluding to the first chapter of Genesis. Genesis 1:27 states that "God created man in his own image, in the image of God he created him; male and female he created them." Since the Bible is the Word of God and speaks only truth, Catholics are convinced this means there is an order to human existence—a way things ought to be. God intended each of us to be either male or female, giving us male or female bodies.

Over the centuries this order has been questioned. In early Christianity the most prevalent heresy was Gnosticism, which taught there was a strict separation between mind and body, spirit and matter. Gnostics believed the spiritual world was good and the material world was bad. Your mind or your soul is good; your body is bad.

It's easy to see a form of Gnosticism behind the transgender movement. Today, people assert that your gender, which is your mental or emotional sense of identity, is what ultimately matters. And they hold that your body, including your biological sex, is malleable and can sometimes conflict with your gender. You even hear people saying they are "trapped in the wrong body," as if their body were some sort of prison. That's Gnostic talk.

In the seventeenth century, René Descartes, a French philosopher, taught that humans are combinations of two different substances, the mind and the body. But according to Descartes, the mind constitutes who you really are as a person (hence his famous adage "I think therefore I am"). The body, according to Descartes, is merely a machine in which the soul exists. So, in a famous phrase, Descartes believed we are all just "ghosts in a machine."

Catholicism rejects both Gnosticism and Descartes's "ghosts in a machine" approach. The Catholic Church, following Aristotle and Thomas Aquinas, teaches that humans are a composite of mind and body. You're not just a mind, and you're not just a body. You are a mind-body, or an embodied mind. Since our gender identity is primarily in our mind, and our sex is determined by our body, and since we are mind-body composites, this means gender and sex are inseparable. They are intrinsically linked, both part of your identity. Thus, the Church objects to modern gender theory that says gender is fluid and chosen, rather than something given by God, such as your body. Our gender identity ought to correspond to our sex, and if our sense of gender conflicts, the problem is not with our body. The problem is with our mind or emotions.

How does the Catholic Church view transgender people? First, the Church sees every person as made in the image of God and as having intrinsic dignity and immeasurable worth. The primary lens through which all Catholics should view anyone struggling with gender issues is as a son or daughter of God.

But what about the moral question? Is transgenderism immoral? Well, as of yet, there are not official Church teachings that say some gender behaviors are sinful and others are not. However, we can deduce some things from other Catholic principles. First, there is nothing sinful with feeling distressed and confused about your gender. Catholic morality holds that sinning requires an act of the will. If something affects you against your will, it is by definition not a sin. Thus, gender dysphoria is not inherently sinful. And feeling you don't fit the stereotypical masculine or feminine categories in your culture is not sinful either. A girl who enjoys sports or a boy who enjoys dancing or painting is not being immoral.

That said, we run into trouble by the way some people respond to their feelings of gender dysphoria. For instance, gender-reassignment surgery *is* definitely problematic. Since our bodies are gifts from God, intentionally damaging them is always a willful assault against God's will and order, which is the definition of sin.

Gender-reassignment surgery damages healthy sexual organs in order to reshape your body according to your preferences. That's immoral, and the Catholic Church rejects it, not only because it distorts the gift of our bodies, but also because it rarely solves the underlying problems of dysphoria and in many cases can make things worse.

Finally, what about cross-dressing, wearing clothes or makeup that presents you as the opposite sex? This is a complex question that's probably best handled between transgender people and their pastor or spiritual director. We should be careful not to make moral judgments about cross-dressing from the outside. There's nothing intrinsically wrong with wearing clothes that are typically associated with the opposite sex, but there are psychological and spiritual concerns with cross-dressing. Some psychologists tell us that it offers a less permanent and dramatic way to deal with gender confusion—a better option than surgery— but still, it rarely solves the root problems of dysphoria and often feeds the disorder rather than resolves it.

They key takeaway is that the Catholic Church is convinced humans are mind-bodies or embodied minds. This means that the gender we identify with in our minds is invariably linked to the biological sex of our bodies. If we have confusion about our gender, the problem is not with our bodies. The problem is with our minds, emotions, or feelings.

The Church's first and last response to people struggling with gender identity issues is always love. If the Church could offer one message to a transgender person, it would be this: "You are a son or daughter of God, created with immeasurable dignity. You were not a mistake, and you are deeply loved."

Expert Interview with Dr. Michelle Cretella

➤ **Watch the interview here: https://claritasu.com/cretella**

Dr. Michelle Cretella is president of the American College of Pediatricians and a general pediatrician with a special interest in behavioral pediatrics. She is one of the college's chief researchers, writers, and spokespersons on issues of pediatric mental and sexual health. She's also an expert in gender dysphoria, especially as it affects children.

In this interview, Cretella responds to the following questions:

1. You've been a pediatrician for many years, but how did you get involved with transgender issues?
2. Should we be concerned that mainstream medical organizations support transgenderism?
3. In a popular article you claim that transgender ideology has produced "large-scale, institutionalized child abuse." Why do you describe it as child abuse?

4. Why are you skeptical of experiments and studies about transgenderism?
5. If someone has a friend or family member who identifies as transgender, what's the best way to relate to them? What should you say to them?

Excerpt from the Interview

"Preschool children are being read picture books that are teaching them they can be trapped in the wrong body. For example, there's one called *Introducing Teddy*. He's a boy bear wearing a bow tie at the beginning of the book, and by the end of the book he has transformed into a girl bear wearing the bow tie as a barrette." (Michelle Cretella)

FIVE QUESTIONS TO ASK TRANSGENDERISM ADVOCATES

When transgender topics come up around the dinner table or water cooler, you should direct the conversation by asking good questions. Questions take the heat and stress off of you and put the other person in the spotlight. They also help you better understand what the other person believes.

Sometimes questions can expose holes in the other people's positions. Maybe they haven't fully wrestled with the conclusions of their view, or maybe they just haven't considered it carefully. In any case, here are five questions that will get transgender supporters thinking:

Question 1: "How do you define transgenderism, gender, and sex?"

There is so much confusion and disagreement about these terms that the first thing you want to do is get clear on how the other person understands them. This will ensure that you're not just talking past each other, wasting your time using the same words in different ways.

Question 2: "Why should we affirm people who feel their gender doesn't match their body, but not people experiencing other forms of bodily dysphoria?"

Here are three examples you can use to frame the conversation.

Black Person "Trapped" in a White Body

Rachel Dolezal was the head of the Spokane NAACP (National Association for the Advancement of Colored People), which advocates for the rights of black people. But last year, Dolezal was discovered to have two white parents. In other words, she is undeniably white, and that made the NAACP upset. While the NAACP does have white leaders, members claimed that Dolezal misled them into thinking she was black.

But instead of apologizing, Dolezal claimed she wasn't sorry, because she actually *is* black. She said, "I feel like the idea of being trans-black would be much more accurate than saying 'I'm white.' Because you know, I'm not white. . . . To say that I'm black is to say, this is how I see the world. . . . Calling myself black feels more accurate than saying I'm white."[6]

Now if a white person feels he or she is really a black person trapped in a white person's body, how should we respond? Should we affirm their identity, or do we recognize that they're confused and offer help instead? Most people would say the latter.

Healthy Person Believes She's Disabled

Chloe Jennings-White, a smart woman with PhDs from Cambridge and Stanford, suffers from body integrity identity disorder (BIID). That's a psychological condition in which healthy people believe they're disabled. To match their disabled identity, they want to damage their normally functioning body, usually by amputating their limbs or becoming paraplegic.

Even though her legs function properly, Jennings-White identifies as disabled and uses leg braces and a wheelchair. In interviews, she has stated that if she had the money, she would have surgery to cut her sciatic and femoral nerves in order to paralyze her legs.

By all appearances, this condition is difficult for her. Living as an able-bodied person is as painful for her as it is for a transgender person to live in accordance with their biological sex. But should we support Chloe's belief that she's disabled? Should we perform surgery to bring her body more in line with her beliefs by damaging her functional body parts? Or should we recognize that she's mentally confused and try to bring her mind and feelings into alignment with her body? Most people would say the latter.

Cat "Trapped" in a Human Body

A young woman named Nano, from Oslo, Norway, claims she is a cat trapped in a human body. This is not a joke. As Nano explained in an interview with a reporter, she genuinely believes she was "born in the wrong species." Now before you think this is fake, there's an actual psychological disorder on the books called species dysphoria. It occurs in people who identify as a nonhuman animal or who have excessive concern that their body is of the wrong species. So, if transgender supporters want to affirm people who believe they were born with the wrong body, why not affirm Nano who believes she was born with the wrong species? Most people won't.

These three examples aren't meant to make fun of gender dysphoria. The point is that for all other forms of bodily dysphoria, we recognize the problem is not with people's bodies. The problem is in their minds. So why treat gender dysphoria differently? Why prescribe reassignment surgery for gender dysphoria but not for transracial, transabled, or trans-species people? Why do we affirm people who experience dysphoria about their gender but not those who experience it about their race, health, height, weight, or other identities? The fact that there are no good answers to these questions should make transgender supporters reconsider their views.

Question 3: "If it's possible for people to be born 'trapped in a body of the wrong sex,' then why don't identical twins of transgender people all identify as transgender?"

Identical twins share 100 percent of the same DNA and are exposed to the same prenatal hormones. So, if genes or prenatal hormones contributed significantly to transgenderism, we should expect both twins to identify as transgender nearly 100 percent of the time.

Yet in the largest study of transgender adults with twin siblings, published by Milton Diamond in 2013, only 28 percent of the identical twins both identified as transgender. In other words, 72 percent of the twins identified differently from their transgender sibling.[7] Studies like this one demonstrate that the belief in innate gender identity or the idea that feminized or masculinized brains can be trapped in the wrong body from before birth is a myth that has no basis in science. So, if someone tries to tell you transgender people were born that way, or born with the wrong sex, ask them about identical-twin studies.

Question 4: "What does it mean to be a man or woman?"

Consider the definition of a woman. Many transgender supporters believe that we can't know whether people are women by simply looking at the person's appearance or anatomy or genes. We can only know someone is a woman by their self-declared gender identity. If they identify as a woman, they're a woman; if they don't, they're not. The only answer to the question "What is a woman?" becomes "a person who identifies as a woman." But this is a circular definition that tells us nothing about what a woman *is*.

Notably, this is why progressive feminists are increasingly at odds with the transgender movement. If the word *woman* is defined as "someone who identifies as a woman," then the word *woman* becomes meaningless. And if the word *woman* loses all meaning, then women as a class disappear, along with all the efforts of feminism to promote women's rights. So even progressive feminists agree that the word *woman* refers to something specific and objective—a person with the biological sex of female.

Question 5: "When individuals feel conflicted about their gender identity, why is the only course of action to bring the body into closer conformity with their psychological state, rather than vice versa?"

If the conflict is mainly psychological—in the mind—why should we recommend invasive surgical procedures to make the body more closely match the mind instead of treatment that might help move the mind closer to their sex? Transgender supporters claim that the only loving response to a transgender person is to affirm their identity and support their desire for medical solutions to fix their bodies. However, as we mentioned above, in 2011 a study of transsexual persons who had reassignment surgery in Sweden revealed suicide rates twenty times higher than the general public. The surgeries didn't seem to solve the underlying dysphoria.

Our entire medical tradition is based on the principle that the purpose of medicine is to *restore* bodily functions and faculties that aren't working properly. So why is it acceptable to say *no* to a trans-abled person who wants surgery to paralyze her limbs but hateful and transphobic to oppose surgeries that damage perfectly functional body parts, such as reproductive organs? This is a tough question for transgender supporters to answer.

These five questions will give you some things to ask supporters of transgenderism and expose the serious holes in their position. You don't have to be put on the spot. You just need to remember a couple of the questions, ask them in a spirit of friendly curiosity, and then sit back and listen.

ANSWERING THE BEST OBJECTIONS

When people ask you tough questions, you need to know the best objections and how to respond. That way, whenever they come up, you won't be nervous and you won't get worried, because you've already heard them and know what to say.

Objection 1: "Did you know that 41 percent of transgender young people have attempted suicide? If you don't affirm them or use their preferred pronoun, you're complicit with all these deaths. You're condemning them to suicide!"

Some suggest that without medical treatment, surgery, lifelong hormone therapy, social acceptance, correct pronoun use, and open bathroom access, transgender people will never be comfortable in their bodies or in society. Consequently, they are at a high risk for suicide, and if we don't make these accommodations, the crime of killing transpeople can be laid at the feet of those who do not affirm these steps.

But this isn't true. To answer this accusation, you should make three points.

Compassion

First, you need to affirm unequivocally how awful it is that so many people attempt suicide, that they feel so isolated, confused, and distraught that they're driven to take their own life. The fact that 41 percent of transgender people attempt suicide should be distressing to everyone. We don't want anyone to commit suicide. So make that clear to the other person. They need to know you're not OK with transgender people committing suicide.

Truth

Second, explain that we can't sacrifice truth just because some people will suffer because of it. For example, if your neighbor genuinely believed he was the president of the United States, you wouldn't help him move into the White House, even if he threatened suicide unless you helped him live out his belief. Similarly, if a man thinks he is a woman, we shouldn't affirm his confusion and pretend he's a woman, just because if we don't, he might harm himself. Instead of playing into his confusion, we need to find healthy ways to help him bring his gender into conformity with his body, as many people suffering with gender dysphoria have done.

Surgery Failures

Third, scientists are finding, more and more, that surgery and social affirmation actually make things worse. Once more, recall the 2011 Sweden study that showed that transgender people who had sex-reassignment surgery had a suicide rate twenty times higher than the general population. That tells us surgery doesn't always solve the underlying issues, which are typically psychological, mental, or emotional.

Objection 2: "Why can't you just call people by their chosen pronoun? It's a basic sign of respect!"

People of goodwill are divided on whether to use the preferred pronoun of people confused about their gender. Some say it's an act of respect; others say it just reinforces a lie and feeds into their delusion. Personally, I prefer not to use pronouns that conflict with reality. I prefer not to call a woman "he" just because she thinks she is a man. But I am OK using a person's preferred *name*. For example, I'd be fine calling a female born with the name Jessica "Jessie," or another name, if that's what she preferred, because names are different than pronouns and are not necessarily tied to a particular sex.

But the short answer to this objection is, "I respect all people, but I don't think affirming something that is false is a sign of respect. I'd be happy to use whatever name that person prefers, but I will not call a person 'she' if he's actually male."

Objection 3: "You reject transgenderism because you're part of the heteronormative culture. You have 'cis privilege' and you have no idea what it's like to be transgender." ("Heteronormative culture" is a society that accepts a heterosexual worldview. And "cis privilege" means your gender identity matches your biological sex.)

This argument pops up in just about every conversation about a hot-button issue: you haven't had an abortion, so you can't possibly understand the subject; you've never struggled with homosexuality, so you're in no position to discuss it; and you don't know what it's like to be a racial minority, so how dare you express your opinion.

When answering, you can affirm that we do live in a heteronormative culture and that, it's true, you have no idea what it's like to be transgender. Most of us are cisgender—our gender identity conforms to our biological sex. But the problem is the implied conclusion, that therefore we can't possibly understand the issue or reasonably discuss it.

When you hear this objection, affirm the true premise but then add that you don't need to have experienced transgenderism to understand that it's a sadly confused position. Experiencing something isn't a prerequisite for seeing its flaws. For instance, most of us have never experienced slavery or murder, but we can understand and argue that those things are wrong.

Objection 4: "Why can't you let people use whatever bathrooms they prefer? It won't affect you, so what's the big deal?"

To respond, you should ask, "Why do we have segregated restrooms and changing rooms in the first place?" The answer is that sex is a morally relevant distinction. Men and women are often sexually attracted to one another. Or at least they experience feelings of discomfort when they are forced to disrobe or perform intimate body functions near one another. Therefore, the common good is best served by segregating men and women in places where disrobing or intimate bodily functions occur.

Of course, one simple solution to this issue is for buildings to offer a single-use or gender-neutral facility that is usually a small, private bathroom or an individual stall that can be used by any person of whatever gender. This alleviates most of the problems. But in cases where installing a single-use bathroom is not possible, we still shouldn't open our restrooms and locker rooms to people based on the gender they identify with.

Objection 5: "You're just a transphobic bigot! You wish transgender people didn't exist!"

First, respond by remaining calm and explaining that you're not transphobic. *Transphobic* describes someone who hates or is afraid of transgender people. But you don't hate them, and you're not afraid of them. You just think they're confused.

Second, you're not a bigot. A bigot is someone who refuses to acknowledge any opinion but their own. Affirm that you're totally open to considering all opinions, but that shouldn't prevent you from opposing them or critically analyzing them.

Finally, affirm that you don't wish transgender people would disappear. You love all people, including transgender people, and believe they have infinite dignity and worth. You don't wish transgender *people* would disappear, but you do wish *gender dysphoria* would go away. Even transgender supporters would agree that gender dysphoria is an awful experience that we should seek to eradicate. We just differ about how best to solve it.

When discussing transgenderism, even with people who vigorously disagree, be sure to approach the conversation in a spirit of peace and compassion. Don't get angry, don't raise your voice, and don't get heated. That will only feed into the perception that your opposition to transgenderism is based in emotions and bigotry. Instead, remain calm, speak slowly and carefully, and be quick to affirm points of agreement.

TIPS FOR TALKING WITH TRANSGENDER PEOPLE

So far, we've covered the issue objectively, but how should you address a friend or family member who is struggling with transgenderism themselves? Let's look at how to handle these sensitive conversations.

As we noted above, transgender people make up 1 to 2 percent of the population. That means you likely already know people experiencing confusion about their gender identity. Those people will increasingly "come out" regarding their transgenderism, which means you should be prepared to talk with them.

Here are seven tips to help you know what to say and how to say it. None of these tips are meant to substitute for professional help. Many transgender people would benefit from consulting counselors, trained therapists, or priests and spiritual directors. Nor are these tips designed to equip you with the necessary skills to "fix" someone's gender struggles. These are just seven good tips to help you have a fruitful discussion with them that will be mutually beneficial and hopefully lead them to the true source of healing, which is Jesus Christ.

Tip 1: Listen to them.

Listen first and ask lots of questions. What do they mean by gender? How do they experience their gender? If they don't think their gender conforms to their body, what's that like? Can they describe it? If the other person says, "You don't understand," say, "That's probably true. So please tell me!"

Tip 2: Empathize with their struggle.

Acknowledge that whatever you each believe about gender, the discomfort they experience is real and painful. For some people, the pain is chronic, going back to early childhood. The emotional agony can feel unbearable. So don't deny this pain. Be sensitive to it, and make sure they know you empathize with their struggle.

If you're talking with someone with gender dysphoria, say something like, "Before we talk further, I know this is a painful and discomforting topic for you. I don't know how it feels, but I can imagine how difficult it must be for you."

Tip 3: Treat them with respect, compassion, and sensitivity.

Those words come directly from the *Catechism of the Catholic Church*. Although the *Catechism* doesn't comment on transgenderism, it does say this about our attitudes toward same-sex attracted people: "They must be accepted with respect, compassion, and sensitivity. Every sign of unjust discrimination in their regard should be avoided" (*CCC*, 2358). These words apply equally well to transgender people. For example, we should stand against bullying of transgender people in any form. You might say something like, "I'm sorry if you've ever been harassed or bullied because of your gender identity. That's appalling and I'm against it. You should always be treated with respect and dignity."

Tip 4: Remind them that their gender does not define them.

We're moving into more delicate waters here, but it's important to communicate the truth about their identity. One difficulty when talking with people today is that so many correlate their beliefs, their sexual orientation, or their gender identity with who they are as a person. Therefore, they think, "If you disagree with my beliefs, you must hate me or reject me as a person."

But this isn't true. Your gender beliefs may be an important part of your identity, but they're not the core of who you are. You need to affirm this. You might say to them, "You're not *a transgender person*. That's not ultimately who you are. That's not what defines you. Your true identity is a beloved child of God, created with inestimable dignity and worth." Remind them they are not reducible to their beliefs or sexual identity. It may be the first time someone's ever said that to them.

Tip 5: Apologize for any ways that Christians have failed them.

Churches should be the safest places to talk about, be open about, and struggle with gender dysphoria. More often than not, however, Christians have made transgender people feel like weirdos, outcasts, and sometimes even worse. So apologize for any way other Christians have hurt or dismissed them, even if you weren't involved. Such an apology is a sign of humility. It will defuse tension and open them up to reconsidering what a Christian like you has to say about gender identity issues.

Tip 6: Show them how Christ can help them.

All of us struggle, in one way or another, with our bodies. We don't like this or that feature, or we feel uncomfortable with this body part. We are never going to find inside ourselves the answer to these body problems. And they won't be found through doctors, surgeons, or therapists, as helpful as all those good people are.

Whatever we might do to our bodies to overcome perceived problems, we'll never be able to repair what truly lies beneath our self-alienation. We can alter our appearance; we can correct much of what we think to be wrong. But we will never find the fix that we so desperately crave. We can't solve it ourselves.

What we need is Jesus Christ. Saint Pope John Paul II loved to say that Jesus "reveals man to himself."[8] He is the perfect man who experienced ultimate brokenness by assuming all the brokenness of the world in order to defuse it and heal us. Bodily brokenness of any kind can point us to the broken body of Christ and, through that brokenness, to the eventual restoration and healing that comes only through him.

Tip 7: Love must animate everything that you say to a transgender person.

Most of us mistake love for a feeling. Or we assume love means just being really nice to someone. This is why you'll often hear people talk about trying to reconcile love with truth, as if they were in competition or mutually exclusive. But as Pope Benedict XVI reminded us in his encyclical *Caritas in Veritate* (Charity in Truth), love and truth go together. They're a package deal. Telling the truth is an act of love, and all loving acts are grounded in the truth of what's good for another person.

This is very important when it comes to transgenderism. Love means to will the good of the other, to pursue what's truly best for them. With that in mind, everything you say and do toward a transgender person should be animated by love. Keep asking yourself, "What's best for this person? How can I will this person's good? What would be good for me to do for this person?"

Notice I didn't say, "What would make the person happy?" or "What would affirm and appease the person?" Love requires sharing difficult truths that won't immediately satisfy the other person.

If you finish a conversation with transgender people and they're unaware that you love them, that you are 100 percent committed to pursuing their good, then you've come up short. That fact must be clear to them. It's the only way they'll be open to hearing what you say and the only hope for them ever changing their minds. So make sure you express love.

RECOMMENDED BOOKS
(in order of importance)

Ryan T. Anderson, *When Harry Became Sally: Responding to the Transgender Moment* (Encounter Books, 2018).

This book is perhaps the only comprehensive Catholic book on transgenderism. Anderson draws on the best insights from biology, psychology, and philosophy to offer a fresh approach to transgender questions. He also shares the personal stories of men and women who tried to transition their gender but found themselves no better off, including children who were encouraged to transition but later regretted it.

Andrew Walker, *God and the Transgender Debate* (The Good Book Company, 2017).

This book unwinds the complexity of transgenderism, gender identity, and gender dysphoria. Walker not only sifts through all of the confusion but also presents it in a refreshingly clear way. He handles a dozen of the toughest questions, including "Can you be transgender and Christian?"

Vaughan Roberts, *Talking Points: Transgender* (The Good Book Company, 2016).

This seventy-five-page booklet is short, accessible, and really cuts to the chase. Roberts takes a theological approach to the issue, using scripture and Christian theology, rather than psychology or psychiatry, as the lens through which to assess transgenderism. The book also has some good definitions of the key terms in the transgender discussion that will help you talk intelligently about the issues.

Mark Yarhouse, *Understanding Gender Dysphoria: Navigating Transgender Issues in a Changing Culture* (IVP Academic, 2015).

Yarhouse is an Evangelical Protestant, a psychology professor, and a licensed clinical psychologist. He focuses especially on the medical side of things, sharing many stories about his experiences counseling transgender people. He engages the latest research while remaining pastorally sensitive to the experiences of each person. In the midst of a tense political climate, Yarhouse calls Christians to come alongside those on the margins and stand with them as they resolve their questions and concerns about gender identity.

FOR REFLECTION AND DISCUSSION

1. If someone asked you to explain the terms *gender identity* and *gender dysphoria*, what would you say?
2. Why do you think the suicide rate is so high among transgendered persons?
3. What reasons does the Catholic Church give for rejecting transgenderism?
4. What might you say to someone who contends that because of your background you have no understanding of what it's like to be transgender?
5. A friend declares that failure to affirm transgendered people condemns them to suicide. How would you correct their view?
6. What advice would you give to someone who wants to speak with a transgendered person about the condition?

FOR PRACTICE

For each of the following scenarios, write a response using what you learned in this chapter.

1. A Facebook friend says to you, "If you oppose transgender people, you obviously don't care about human life. Aren't you supposed to be pro-life? Transgender people are committing suicide because people like you won't let them be who they are." (Respond with at least two points and ask a question.)

2. A colleague tells you, "Transgender is not a choice. People are born that way. They are born into the wrong body, and this is shown by brain scans that confirm they have a brain resembling the opposite gender. Based on this scientific fact, everyone should support reassignment surgery." (Respond with material from the chapter and ask a question.)

CONCLUSION

As we noted at the beginning, most Catholics are terrified to discuss these issues. They'd prefer to ignore them. But now, having finished this book, you're different. Even if you haven't memorized every tactic and talking point, you're still ready to discuss these topics without getting nervous or scared. You know the key points, you've heard the top objections, and you've seen how to answer them. You have clarity, and remember: clarity breeds confidence.

However, you likely still need two things to move forward. First, you need a place where you can practice these strategies. It's one thing to read about them in a book. It's a whole different thing to master them and use them in the real world, in actual conversations. That's why inside ClaritasU we have a Community area, with several discussion forums, where you can join thousands of other Catholics in practicing these skills, asking questions and getting feedback. It's like a training ground for Catholics wanting to master the skills in this book.

Second, you need to stay up to date on new topics and challenges that arise. Developments in the culture often change how we should approach each of these issues, so you want to make sure you have the latest information and the most effective tactics. You'll also want to get knowledgeable about new challenges, ones we haven't covered in this book.

Again, that's what you'll find inside ClaritasU. Each week students receive a new video lesson from me, and every couple of months, we begin a new video course on a burning issue, which means you'll never be left with old, outdated information. You'll always be on the cutting edge. You'll know what to say, and how to say it, about all the most important topics.

So, as we finish this book, I invite you to join me and thousands of other Catholics inside ClaritasU. Join this movement of excited Catholics rising up against timidity and fear, and gain the confidence and clarity you need.

Visit ClaritasU.com and sign up today. See you inside!

ACKNOWLEDGMENTS

I'd like to thank Ave Maria Press for partnering with me and ClaritasU on this book and for believing in the need for a New Apologetics. You continue to raise the bar for excellence in Catholic publishing.

Special gratitude also goes to Bert Ghezzi, my tireless friend and editor. Without your affirmation, I never would have written my first book, much less this one. Thank you for shaping each of my books into something coherent and readable.

Thank you to John DeRosa, a constant source of joy and encouragement. You've done so much to help the ClaritasU community, especially through your astute comments, your video editing, and the excellent workbooks you compile for each course. Between ClaritasU and your own projects, you're doing so much good for the Church.

Most important, I'd like to thank the more than four thousand members of the ClaritasU community who helped inspire this book and have refined many of the tactics and ideas. You're on the front lines of the New Evangelization, and I'm grateful to be your partner on this missionary adventure.

NOTES

1. Answering Atheism

1. As quoted in Wesley C. Salmon, "Religion and Science: A New Look at Hume's Dialogues," *Philosophical Studies 33*, no. 2 (1978): 176.

2. Alexander Vilenkin, cited in Lisa Grossman, "Why Physicists Can't Avoid a Creation Event," *New Scientist*, January 11, 2012.

3. Richard Dawkins, *River out of Eden: A Darwinian View of Life* (New York: Basic, 1995), 133.

2. Evil and Suffering

1. David Hume, *Dialogues Concerning Natural Religion* (Boston: Agora Publications, 2004), 119.

2. See Trent Horn, *Answering Atheism: How to Make the Case for God with Logic and Charity* (San Diego: Catholic Answers, 2013), 77–107.

3. C. S. Lewis, *The Problem of Pain* (New York: HarperOne, 2015), 92.

4. John Loftus, *Why I Became an Atheist: A Former Preacher Rejects Christianity* (New York: Prometheus Books, 2012), 240–241.

5. Augustine, *On Free Choice of the Will* (Indianapolis: Hackett Publishing Company, 1993), 81.

3. Trusting the Gospels

1. *Catechism of the Catholic Church*, 101.

2. Bart D. Ehrman, *Misquoting Jesus: The Story behind Who Changed the Bible and Why* (New York: HarperSanFrancisco, 2005), 10.

3. Craig Blomberg, *Can We Still Believe the Bible? An Evangelical Engagement with Contemporary Questions* (Grand Rapids, MI: Brazos, 2014), 27.

4. Ehrman, *Misquoting Jesus*, 252.

5. Brant Pitre, *The Case for Jesus: The Biblical and Historical Evidence for Christ* (New York: Image, 2016), 71–77.

6. Quoted in Pitre, *Case for Jesus*, 74.

7. Quoted in Pitre, *Case for Jesus*, 75.

8. Pitre, *Case for Jesus*, 76.

4. Explaining the Eucharist

1. Ignatius of Antioch, *Epistle to the Smyraeans* 7, http://www.newadvent.org/fathers/0109.htm. Language slightly adapted to modern English.

2. Ignatius of Antioch, *Letter to the Romans* 7:3, http://www.newadvent.org/fathers/0107.htm. Language slightly adapted to modern English.

3. Justin Martyr, *First Apology* 66, http://www.newadvent.org/fathers/0126.htm. Language slightly adapted to modern English.

4. Irenaeus of Lyons, *Against Heresies* (n.p.: Ex Fontibus, 2012), 512.

5. *Luther's Collected Works*, Wittenburg Edition, no. 7 p, 391. Quoted at https://bfhu.wordpress.com/2011/05/13/martin-luther-on-the-real-presence.

5. Abortion

1. Doe v. Bolton, 410 US 179 (1973).

2. Adapted from Trent Horn, *Persuasive Pro-Life: How to Talk about Our Culture's Toughest Issue* (El Cajon, CA: Catholic Answers Press, 2014), 68.

6. Same-Sex Marriage

1. "Attitudes on Same-Sex Marriage," Pew Research Center, May 14, 2019, https://www.pewforum.org/fact-sheet/changing-attitudes-on-gay-marriage.

7. Transgenderism

1. "Gender Identity," YouTube, January 25, 2018, https://www.youtube.com/watch?v=xfO1veFs6Ho.

2. Ariel Levy, "Dolls and Feelings," *New Yorker*, December 6, 2015.

3. Katherine Kersten, "Transgender Conformity at Nova Classical Academy," Center of the American Experiment, November 10, 2016, https://www.americanexperiment.org/article/transgender-conformity-nova-classical-academy.

4. See "Know Your Rights: Health Care," National Center for Transgender Equality, accessed December 6, 2019, https://transequality.org/know-your-rights/health-care.

5. Pope Francis, "Address of His Holiness Pope Francis," July 27, 2016, http://www.vatican.va/content/francesco/en/speeches/2016/july/documents/papa-francesco_20160727_polonia-vescovi.html.

6. Decca Aitkenhead, "Rachel Dolezal: 'I'm Not Going to Stoop and Apologise and Grovel,'" *Guardian*, February 25, 2017, https://www.theguardian.com/us-news/2017/feb/25/rachel-dolezal-not-going-stoop-apologise-grovel.

7. Milton Diamond, "Transexuality among Twins: Identity Concordance, Transition, Rearing, and Orientation," *International Journal of Transgenderism* 14 (2013): 24–38.

8. John Paul II, *Redemptor Hominis* (The Redeemer of Man), March 4, 1979, http://www.vatican.va/content/john-paul-ii/en/encyclicals/documents/hf_jp-ii_enc_04031979_redemptor-hominis.html.

Brandon Vogt is a best-selling and award-winning author, blogger, and speaker who serves as content director for Bishop Robert Barron's Word on Fire Catholic Ministries.

Vogt was one of the millennial "nones" when it came to religion until, as a mechanical engineering student at Florida State University, he began a passionate search for truth. That search led him unexpectedly to the Catholic Church in 2008. In 2013, he started StrangeNotions.com, the largest site of dialogue between Catholics and atheists.

Vogt was named one of the "Top 30 Catholics under 30" by FOCUS as well as one of the "Top 30 Catholics to Follow on Twitter." He is the author of seven books, including *RETURN: How to Draw Your Child Back to the Church* and *The Church and New Media*. *Why I Am Catholic (and You Should Be Too)* won first place in the 2018 Catholic Press Association book awards for popular presentation of the faith. His work has been featured by media outlets, including NPR, Fox News, CBS, EWTN, *America* magazine, Vatican Radio, *Our Sunday Visitor*, *National Review*, and *Christianity Today*. He is a regular guest on Catholic radio and speaks to a variety of audiences about evangelization, new media, Catholic social teaching, and spirituality.

www.brandonvogt.com
www.claritasu.com
strangenotions.com

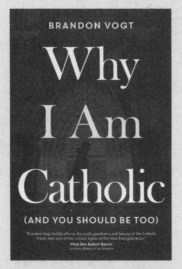